W9-CNR-656

A Journey Through Your Childhood

Also by Christopher Biffle:

The Castle of the Pearl: A Guide to Self-Knowledge
A Guided Tour of Five Works by Plato
A Guided Tour of Rene Descartes' Meditations on First Philosophy
A Guided Tour of Aristotle's Nicomachean Ethics (Fall 1989)
A Guided Tour of David Hume's Dialogues Concerning Natural Religion (Fall 1989)
Time Throttle: An Electronic Atlas of Western Culture (software and book, Fall 1989)
Garden in the Snowy Mountains: An Inner Journey with Christ as Your Guide (Fall 1989)

A JOURNEY THROUGH YOUR CHILDHOOD

A Write-In Guide for Reliving Your Past, Clarifying Your Present, and Charting Your Future

CHRISTOPHER BIFFLE

Illustrations by Mary Nadler

JEREMY P. TARCHER, INC.
Los Angeles

Library of Congress Cataloging in Publication Data

Biffle, Christopher.
A journey through your childhood: a write-in guide for reliving your past, clarifying your present, and charting your future/Christopher Biffle.
p. cm.
ISBN 0-87477-499-3
1. Reminiscing—Problems, exercises, etc. 2. Emotions in children—Problems, exercises, etc. 3. Self-actualization (Psychology)—Problems, exercises, etc. I. Title.
BF378.R44B54 1988 88-31132
158′.1—dc19 CIP

Jeremy P. Tarcher, Inc.
9110 Sunset Blvd.
Los Angeles, CA 90069

Distributed by St. Martin's Press, New York

Illustrations by Mary Nadler

Design by Tanya Maiboroda

Manufactured in the United States of America
10 9 8 7 6 5 4 3 2 1

First Edition

This book is dedicated to my beloved wife, Deidre:
¡O, corazón de mi corazón, alma de mi alma, tenemos dos vidas para Dios!

CONTENTS

Introduction: The Pleasures of Going Home 1

1. How to Remember 5

2. A Season Within Childhood 12

PART 1

THE OUTER WORLD OF CHILDHOOD

3. A Vivid Memory of Home 19

4. The Memories Return 26

5. At Home 30

6. Old Toys 37

7. The Windows of Childhood 41

8. Home Exactly the Way You Remember It 44

9. Walking the Neighborhood 48

10. A Map of the World of Childhood 51

11. The World of Play 54

12. More Memory Locations 60

13. School 63

14. Silent Reverie 69

PART 2

THE INNER WORLD OF CHILDHOOD

15. Memory Photographs 79

16. Life with Parents 87

17. A Family Portrait 98

18. A Wisdom Meditation 103

19. A Child Thinks About the World 113

20. A Child Dreams 117

21. Interlude: The Missing Pieces 122

22. Old Lessons of Childhood 125

23. New Lessons from Childhood 134

24. Painful Memories 137

25. The Wisdom Letter 142

26. The Time Compass 146

Appendix A: For Writing Teachers 151

Appendix B: For Fiction Writers 153

Appendix C: For Therapists 155

"Oh the happy, happy, never-to-be-recalled days of childhood! How could one fail to love and cherish memories of such a time? Those memories refresh and elevate the soul and are a source of my best enjoyment."

Childhood, Boyhood and Youth, Leo Tolstoy

A Journey Through Your Childhood

INTRODUCTION

THE PLEASURES OF GOING HOME

We return Home after a long absence, just to be there, to feel old emotions again, to wander about the place, and to recapture who we were long ago. We also return to discover who we have become. We go back to our beginning to see our present more clearly. Learning this, perhaps we can find the best way into the future.

This book will take us both home again. Like a game of follow-the-leader, you fill in the blanks and do what I do. Together we will relive our childhoods, clarify our present lives, and chart our futures.

I don't want to merely think about my childhood. I want, as much as words, memory, and emotion will allow, to return to it. I don't want to escape into childhood. I simply want to touch it again. I want to play with old toys. I want the pleasure of homecoming.

I also want Wisdom. I'd like to know what my mother and father taught me about myself and my world that shaped my life. I'd like to look at myself again and see what kind of boy I was. I want to know what was healthy and harmful in my heart thirty-five years ago. I want to go back in order to go forward.

However, I don't want to remember in order to suffer. This journey is not psychoanalytic; it is nostalgic. For most people, it was good to be a child, if only in comparison to the life of hard work that lay ahead. Long ago we played as we never would play again. We had few worries and few responsibilities. It was great to get up in the morning and know that the worst that could happen was mowing the lawn.

I am not saying childhood lacked terrors. I am not presuming that every reader lived in bliss. There is childhood pain I want to learn from, but only after I have built a world of play around it.

In this book I have constructed a journey for almost anyone who wishes to go, even for those whose past held hardship or difficulty. The pain of childhood is saved for one chapter near the end of the book, and that chapter may be skipped. However, if the idea of returning to your childhood produces far more negative than positive emotions, this book is not for you. I especially do not recommend this journey if you were abused physically or sexually as a child. A book is not a satisfactory way to deal with a series of terrible memories.

I include my own memories in the following chapters simply to give you a model and impetus for recording and analyzing your own. They may remind you of something similar in your childhood or of something different. As we proceed further on the journey, and as you gain skill in creating your own memoir, there will be less about me and more about you.

At first, filling in blanks and completing sentences may seem too simple. But the best beginning *is* the simplest; this journey should be easy, not hard. We are going back to have fun, not to labor. Fill in the blanks with the first words that occur to you; relax, enjoy yourself. Do not turn this into work. Soon you will be making surprising discoveries. Everything you need to know is already inside you.

Think of our journey together as a conversation. First I talk about my past, and then you talk about yours. Let the conversation between us flow; both the similarities and the differences between our childhoods will produce memories for you.

Don't be limited by the blank lines in this book. If you decide to extend your recollections into a journal, you may end up with a complete autobiography. In fact, my wife insists that one of the most rewarding uses of this book is to pass it on to your children or grandchildren. What would you be willing to give to read your parents' version of this journey into their childhood?

Together, we are going to re-create the world we lived in during a particular season in the place we remember, more than any other, as Home. In the first half of this book, the Outer World of Childhood, we will walk through rooms at Home, play with old toys, recall important places in the neighborhood, revisit our old school. Each chapter adds to the previous one until, little by little, a complete portrait of a season of our youth emerges. At the end of this section, we will have a detailed map of this Outer World of Childhood. We will be ready for a Silent Reverie in which we relive our childhood in detail.

In the second half of this book, the Inner World of Childhood, we are ready to search for personal Wisdom. *Personal Wisdom* may be briefly defined at this point as revelatory knowledge about ourselves and/or our world. We don't simply want knowledge about our past; we want revealing knowledge that casts a light in important, unexpected ways. Thus, in the second half of this book, we carefully explore the feelings that churned through our hearts long ago. We think in detail about our parents, ourselves, and our crucial experiences at Home. We ask, once again, the great questions of childhood and discover the implicit and explicit answers our parents gave us. We will try to see clearly what we were taught about our character, the world, the goal of life, and the nature of love. We will investigate our parents' conceptions of those two powerful models we still have with us, the Good Person and the Bad Person. In essence, we seek Wisdom about the ideas and experiences that shaped our present personality.

At the end of our journey, you will find a gift, the Time Compass, to guide you on additional explorations of your past. I have also included appendices describing how this book can be used by writing teachers, fiction writers, and therapists.

We will start with the easiest techniques for remembering the past.

·1· How to Remember

There's nothing like old pictures to trigger memories. I have a photograph of my father and me and a friend at the zoo. The bill of my baseball cap is turned up. My father is wearing an overcoat; I can feel the texture of that coat right now, against my palm. Ricky, my childhood chum, is eating popcorn, and we are all leaning against the iron fence of the polar bear enclosure. Looking at that picture, I remember suddenly that the most fun thing in the world was a footrace with my father.

Thus, my first advice to help you remember your childhood is to look at old photographs now and at any time on our journey when they would be useful.

Tell me about one favorite picture from your childhood. If you don't have it nearby, describe it from memory.

I have a picture of ______________________________

______________________________. When I look at it I feel ________

______________________________. I remember ____

____

______________________________.

My father kept a third-grade picture of me in his wallet until the day he died. I had been experimenting with scissors and had chopped a hunk out of the front of my hair. In addition, I had a black crayon stripe across my forehead; apparently, both teacher and photographer were too busy to notice. I look like a wonderfully bad boy. Remembering that lad, I recall how good it was to yell and play soldiers and to wonder which was better, a revolver or an automatic.

Throughout our journey, I'd like you to use my memories to spark your own. Pretend that we are two old friends. As I tell about my childhood, you can't wait to tell me about yours.

Now try another photo.

I am thinking now of a picture of myself when I was ____________________

____________________ . I look ______________________________________

____ .

I was the kind of kid who ____

____ .

I want us both to cross over the line between memory and reliving. We don't want merely to remember what our life was like long ago, we want to feel it once again.

One more picture: I am standing on the front lawn with my new bike. I am wearing a plaid shirt and jeans with thick cuffs. The bike has a big basket. I remember pedaling home from the store with a half gallon of milk and a loaf of bread. Right now, I feel exactly how heavy and awkward the bike was to steer.

Describe another picture, and then let it come to life. Use your photo album if that helps.

The picture is ____ .

Thinking back, I remember __________________________________

____ . And this memory leads me to

____

____ .

The childhood emotion I feel right now is ________________________

____

____

____ .

As you begin your journey, please remember that we are not going back into the past to suffer. There is a chapter for pain, but that is far ahead on the journey. For now, divide everything in your childhood into two parts: the pleasurable and the painful. Nine-tenths of this book is about the pleasurable. The portion about the painful can be skipped if you wish. This is your journey. Do what is best for you.

Another good way to remember childhood is to hunt around your house for childhood treasures. As a boy, I swore I would keep my best toys to give to my children because my mother and father had not done that. I have two daughters, and all I have for them is my old .22. Right now, I see that a boy who grew up in the '50s was a real militarist! Looking at my old rifle, I remember the evening my father bought it for me. The gun was used, and the man who sold it to us let me shoot it at a target in his basement. I loved that rifle in a way that I may never have loved any other possession.

When I think of any possessions that take me back to childhood, I think

of ______________________________ . What it meant to me long ago

was ____

____ .

The memories it brings back are ______________________________

____

____ .

Now I feel ____

____ .

Obviously, there are other ways to augment the journey ahead besides looking at photographs and thinking about childhood possessions. Talk to old friends. Ask your parents questions about your childhood. Go through school archives. Look at yearbooks. Search family documents. Ask relatives to tell you about yourself as a child. Listen to records that bring back the past. Or just lie in bed at night and let yourself drift back into childhood.

One of the simplest and most useful memory devices is to make lists. For example, I can list other photographs I could have used in this chapter:

1. Me in my "Lemay Aces" baseball uniform.
2. Eddie Nash and I throwing snowballs
3. The team picture when I was in Little League . . . as a matter of fact, I hadn't thought of this picture in years. I expected to make a longer list before I came to a surprise.

Your turn.

Here is my list of photographs: ______________________________

____

____

____

____.

You may want to start a journal now by writing about the memories and feelings these photos bring forth.

Free association, a technique long used in psychology, can be another useful way to recover the past. The key in free associating is not to filter your responses. Don't look for a "right" association. The first thing that comes to mind is often the most important. For example, what is the very first thing you think of when I say the word *mother*?

"I think of ______________________," you immediately respond.

Here is a list of four important words. Write the first word or phrase that comes to mind. Don't hesitate.

Father ____

Home ____

Toys ____

Dreams ____

Free association can often lead to surprising results. Whenever you get an association that makes you scratch your head and ask, "Now, why did I say that?" you may be on the track of a hidden memory.

Think about the surprising association. Be patient. Play with it. Associate other words or feelings with the ones you already have. Remember, you have the answer somewhere inside. Suddenly, perhaps while you're washing the dishes or walking the dog, the hidden memory will spring into your mind. You have found something long lost, a new treasure to add to your store of memories. Write it down so that you don't lose it again.

Try using free association whenever you come to a blank wall on the journey ahead. As with any other skill, practice will improve your ability.

A second psychological technique for recovering memories is visualization. Carl Jung encouraged his patients to let their dream and fantasy images come alive. He called this "active imagination." As far as I can tell, he limited the concept to one sense: sight.

If it weren't such an awkward word, I would encourage you to practice "multisensualization." One way to go beyond remembering, to reliving, is to add other senses besides sight to your memories. Let's say you have a fairly clear visual image of a room at Home. You can significantly expand this image by recalling sounds, textures, and odors. Let the memory come alive. Don't just see your living room. Walk around inside it and run your hand over the sofa. Listen for sounds outside the door. Walk over and look out the window. Go into the kitchen, lift the lid of the simmering pot, and *inhale.* All this takes practice, but improving your ability to remember, making your memories multisensory and vivid, is part of what this journey is all about.

One final suggestion to aid your memory on the journey ahead: Select the right time and best surroundings for writing and reflecting. Be self-indulgent. I have a favorite English fountain pen and hardcover, handbound journals to write in. On the wall is a map of medieval England (which, for some reason, sets my memories flowing). On my desk are a tin of French hard candies and an egg-shaped piece of polished blue agate.

Find the place, time, and situation when memory speaks the clearest. Build yourself a world that helps you dream about the past.

If I could create the perfect environment for writing and reflecting, it

would have ____

____

____

____

____.

Do whatever you need to do to prepare for your departure into childhood. Unlike most trips, the further you go on this journey, the more energy you will have and the easier it will become. As you add more memories, it will become simpler for you to enter your living childhood. Then, knowing yourself more clearly as a child, you will see more clearly who you are now and who you want to become.

In the next chapter, we select our first destination within childhood.

·2· A Season Within Childhood

I want to go back to St. Louis in the summer of 1954, when I was eight years old, and walk around inside the brick house on Devonshire. I want to play with my Lincoln Logs, sort through my baseball cards, go downstairs, and look into my father's young face when he comes home from the hat factory. I would like to sit in my mother's lap in the family room and sip a glass of Coca-Cola while she talks to her friends. It would be good to go out in the backyard, climb up into my treehouse and safely look over at the black German shepherd who was the terror of the neighborhood. I'd like to sit in that treehouse with my little yellow-handled pocketknife and sharpen sticks. Or I would like to just stand and look out my bedroom window on a Saturday morning, with a new fifty-cent piece in my back pocket, and know I had nothing to do for the rest of the day but play.

This time and place is one of the easiest for me to remember because it was the last summer before my parents divorced. A good world ended then. I was just out of the third grade, and in every direction the horizon was bright.

One useful way to select a particular time from your childhood to revisit, if none immediately occurs to you, is to think of a particular year in grade school and then a season in that year. Perhaps several years blur together; don't worry. Select the house you lived in that was, more than any other, Home. Then let the memories return.

Here is the outline of the childhood world I'm going to re-create.

Season and year: Summer 1954

Place: St. Louis, Missouri

Age: 8

Grade: Third

Home: A two-story brick house on Devonshire, next to a creek; my bedroom on the second floor in the back; one-car garage

Friends: Eddie Nash, my goofy next-door neighbor; Casey (I think that was his name), the older boy who baby-sat me; a girl on the next block (Sharon?)

Possessions: A brown bike with red fenders; a yellow-handled pocketknife; Lincoln Logs and Erector set; baseball cards by the thousands

This is great already. I hadn't thought of that pocketknife until I began writing this chapter, or that brown, battered bike, or my Erector set. We are both in for some surprising memories.

Your turn. What time and place from childhood do you want to re-create and then relive?

I am thinking about ____________________________________

____________________________________. I would like to go back to this

particular time because ____________________________________

____________________________________.

Fill in anything in the following section that seems useful. Don't hurry. The memories will return.

The Time from Childhood I Want to Relive

Season and year: ______________________________

Place: ______________________________

Age: ______________________________

Grade: ______________________________

Home: ______________________________

____

____

____

____

Friends: ______________________________

____

____

____

____

Possessions: ____

____

____

____

Now we are ready to make our first attempt at going beyond remembering childhood to reliving it.

PART • 1

THE OUTER WORLD OF CHILDHOOD

·3·
A Vivid Memory of Home

Let me distinguish more clearly between remembering and reliving childhood. I *remember* sitting in my treehouse, whittling sticks, and looking out over the neighborhood. But I have the feeling that the treehouse and the boy who sat there are part of a distant world. When I *relive* that experience, I feel the ache in my knees from squatting on the plywood floor; I rub my hand across the top of my head and feel a crew cut; I hear the slippery sound that my knife makes against the sapling I sharpen. When I *remember* the past I see it dimly, at arm's distance; when I *relive* the past, sight becomes more vivid and may combine with hearing, touch, and smell. Rather than staring at an image from the past, I can enter the memory and move around inside it.

Throughout this book we start by remembering a particular experience as clearly as possible and end by trying to relive it. I will show you how to do this in a variety of ways. As I said earlier, practice will improve your skill.

I don't want you to think that the movement from remembering to reliving is unusual. You do it all the time. Thinking about a pleasant experience in childhood, for example, you find yourself feeling the same happy emotions. When you remember a Christmas, the memory is dim at first and then, as you focus on it longer, you might be able to feel the crinkly wrapping paper under your hands, or clearly see the gold foil star on top of the tree, or even smell the ham in the oven. A brain scientist might be able to tell us in what physiological sense our memories are buried and how, as they return, they become more real. One value of this journey is that it provides a more structured way to do what we do naturally every time we have vivid recall.

In this chapter we will start with a simple list of perhaps half a dozen memories of life at Home. Then we will select one particularly clear memory from our list and briefly expand it. Finally, we will let the memory come to life and see where it leads us. Doing this will give us the pleasure of returning Home.

Here is a short list of my memories from the house on Devonshire:

1. Learning to ride a bike on the driveway
2. Playing down in the creek
3. Sitting at the breakfast bar
4. Climbing the tree behind the house
5. Sitting on the stairs to the second floor late at night
6. Punching my Joe Palooka punching bag

Now, tell me your list.

I remember ______________________________

____

____

____

____

____

____

The next step is to select the easiest memory to begin with. A good phrase to start with to expand a memory is, "I remember when . . ." Then see what happens.

I will pick the fifth memory on my list because it seems the most interesting. I remember when I would sit on the stairs leading up to my bedroom after bedtime and listen to my parents in the living room downstairs. Creeping down the stairwell, I could see the reflection of the TV in a window above the breakfast bar. I remember sitting there in secrecy and being stunned that I was not discovered.

Now it's your turn.

I will pick ________________________________ because ________

____.

I remember when ____

____

____

____.

Let's add a few more details before we take this one step further. We want the richest possible experience of childhood; we want, for a few moments, to go Home again.

Bring your memory back and describe what else you can see, hear, feel, or smell. For example, if I turn around, I look up the stairs into darkness. I can make out the pattern of small blue flowers on the wallpaper. Now I hear Uncle Miltie on TV!

Visual details I could add to my memory are ______________________

____

______________________________ . I reach out my hand and touch

________________________ . It feels ________________________

______________________________ . One other detail I could add is

____

____ .

Now I'm going back to sit on those stairs again. It is not as difficult as you may think. I will do this in four separate steps. First, I will write about what I see, hear, and feel when I look around on the steps; then I'll describe what is happening; next I'll describe what emotions I feel; finally, I will take some action. I will write without worrying whether my writing is good or bad or going anywhere important. Whenever I am stuck, I will use techniques such as free association, visualization, or looking at photographs to spark my memory.

> I am sitting on the stairs in my parents' house on Devonshire and I am eight years old. Looking behind me I see the dark hall. Below is the reflection of the black-and-white TV in the window. I think there is wallpaper with small blue and white flowers on the walls. I have on flannel pajamas and they feel soft under my hand. I can't hear my parents talking. Maybe Milton Berle is on TV. No! I hear a commercial for Texaco. I feel safe and strangely happy. Now what do I want to do? I hear someone open a soda bottle. I run back upstairs to bed and call my mother, "Mom! Can I have some?"

I hear them laughing. Maybe they make some remark about my wondrous hearing. My dad says I can come downstairs and drink one glass before going back to bed. I run downstairs in delight.

Now, your turn. Let the memory return and come to life.

A First Attempt at Reliving A Vivid Memory from Childhood

This year is ______________________ . I am __________ years old.

Where I am at Home is ____

________________ . The time of day must be about ______________

________________ . I look around and see _____________________

____

____

________________ . I hear ____________________________________

____ .

The emotions I feel are ______________________________________

____

______________________ . What is happening is ________________

____

______________ . What I decide to do is ______________________________

____

____

____

____

____

____

____ .

As I said at the beginning, we have two purposes: to go back to childhood simply for the fun of it, and also to find personal Wisdom.

We seek Wisdom about both the present and the future. On this occasion, just think about the present. What similarities and differences do you see between the child you wrote about and yourself now? Take your time. On this journey there are no clocks.

Some interesting similarities are ______________________________

____

____

____

____

____ .

Some interesting differences are ______________________________

____

____

____

____

____ .

A good definition of personal Wisdom would be anything worth remembering. Wherever on your journey you discover something that seems especially wise, especially worth remembering, place a star beside it. This is one of those fine occasions in life when quality is more important than quantity. A few solitary stars may be more valuable than a galaxy.

·4·
The Memories Return

Now, instead of focusing on one memory, we will try letting one memory lead to another.

I have a whole series of small memories of Home. I remember sitting at the breakfast bar and looking at the black Kit-Kat clock on the wall. Every second, his eyes swung one way and his tail another.

I remember teasing my dog, Brownie, by holding his back legs in a mean way when he wanted to eat his bowl of dog food. We were in the door between the family room and the garage.

I remember the yellow rattan furniture with the big, curving cane arms that my mother had put in the family room. The cushions had green and yellow floral prints. I remember our telephone prefix was ST for Sterling. I loved that word because my mother made sterling silver jewelry.

What do you remember?

I remember ____

____

and I remember ______________________________________

____ .

I'll never forget when ____

________________________ . I also remember ____________________

____

__________________________ . For some reason I also remember ____

____

____ .

Let's go back again. I'm going to put some of my memories together. Follow the same four steps as in the last chapter: Look around and then add information about what you can hear, feel, or smell; describe what is happening; record your emotions; and then take some action.

> It is 1954. I am downstairs in the Devonshire house sitting at the breakfast bar eating Post Toasties from one of those miniature boxes of cereal. I'm drinking milk from an aluminum cup that cottage cheese came in. The cup is bright red and feels cold in my hand. I hear birds chirping outside, but there is no other sound. It is pleasant to be up in the morning before anyone else. I feel good, happy.
>
> I look closely at the Kit-Kat clock. He has no tail. My mother replaced his tail with one bent from a coat hanger. I see the mobile! It is hanging in the family room. My mother made the gossamer thing from string and parts of coat hanger and bits of colored wood. It is so finely balanced that it turns forever.
>
> I look into the family room. The yellow arms of the rattan furniture. A glass-topped coffee table. The dark walls above the sofa. My parents are still asleep upstairs. I go out in the back and call Brownie. He comes running. I pet him. I go get a can of dog food

and feed him. I don't bother him. I watch him eat and tell him he is a good dog.

That mobile was one of the wonders of my childhood, and I hadn't thought about it for thirty-five years. Now it is mine again. One of the lovely things that happens as we return to childhood is making such discoveries. Normally when we think of the past we think the same thoughts over and over again. On this journey we may discover memories that have been lost for decades.

Do what I did and see what you can find. First, look around and add information from your other senses; then describe what is happening; then decide how you feel; finally, take some action. Here, as elsewhere in this book, if you're having trouble remembering, go back to chapter 1 for some tips.

A Second Attempt at Reliving My Childhood

The year is __________ . I am ______________ years old. The room I am in is ____

____

______________________________ . I look around and see _________

____

______________________________ . I also see ___________________

____

____

______________________________ . I hear (or feel or smell) _______

____

____.

What I am doing is ________________________________

____

____

______________________________. Emotionally I feel ______

____

____

____

______________________. Now, what happens is ____________

____

____

____

____

____

____

____.

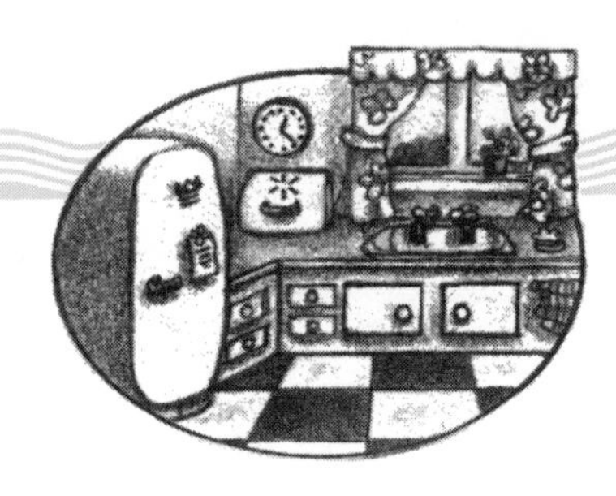

·5·
AT HOME

In this and the next eight short chapters we will continue to fit together, piece by piece, a season in our childhoods. Work as slowly and carefully as you did on those long rainy afternoons when you put together picture puzzles. Memories will return.

Now we will take a walk through the rooms at Home. First I will make a list of each room.

Downstairs

1. Bathroom
2. Washroom in the hallway
3. Kitchen
4. Living room/family room
5. Garage

Upstairs

1. My bedroom
2. The upstairs living room
3. My parents' bedroom

4. Bathroom
5. "Sewing" room (really a storage room)

Now do the same thing. Start with the room that is the clearest in memory.

The rooms I remember are ______________________________

____

____

____

____

____

____

____

____

Spend some time looking at your list. Make notes in the margins about your clearest memories of what was in these rooms. What colors do you see? Textures? How did the couch feel under your hand? The walls? The old chair? What felt cool or smooth or rough? What smells do you remember? Can you remember the different way each room smelled? Was there wallpaper? What were the designs? In what room did you spend the most time?

I remember ______________________________________

Note which rooms your strongest memories come from. These rooms will be the best place to try reliving parts of your childhood later on the tour. What pieces of furniture can you remember? Were there pictures on the walls? What areas or objects in the house were forbidden to you? Where did you play with your toys? Do you remember crying about something in one of the rooms? Or laughing? Or being angry? Or feeling very close to your mother or father, brothers or sisters?

Now I remember ______________________________

Can you remember rugs or linoleum or what the floor looked like in any of the rooms? Where were your favorite hiding places? What small objects or knickknacks do you remember on shelves or tables? What were your parents' treasures? Where was the radio or television set?

Your questions remind me of ______________________________

Now I will walk through the rooms at Home, writing down everything I see (except toys—they need a separate chapter).

Here is a list of what I see in each room.

Walking Through My Home

1. Garage
   Joe Palooka punching bag
   parents' stone-cutting machines
   red ball hanging from garage door for batting practice
2. Family room
   rattan couch
   two rattan armchairs

black telephone
television with funny rabbit ears in corner

3. Kitchen
   huge radio (taller than I am)
   rolls of coins under breakfast bar
   red tile floors
   white, round-shouldered refrigerator
   trash under sink
   chest of drawers (blue, brown?) in hall next to bathroom
4. Living room upstairs
   bare wood floors
   sofa, two chairs
5. My bedroom
   I can see almost nothing here—frustrating
6. Parents' bedroom
   white bedspread
7. Sewing room
   clutter
   sewing machine
   tracing paper
   red pincushion shaped like a tomato
   Mom's jewelry wrapped in white Kleenex in a Whitman's chocolate box
8. Odds and ends
   my mother's box of cut stones
   jade bookends
   washer and dryer in the hall
   something made of wrought iron—the coffee table?

The main problem I have in recalling my bedroom on Devonshire is that I can't untangle it from all the other bedrooms I had afterward. I don't think I spent much time there, except to sleep. Right now I remember a desk in my bedroom in front of the window; I can remember a game spread out on the desktop.

Your turn. Go back Home, walk through each room, and list what you see.

A List of What I See in Each Room at Home

·6· OLD TOYS

Imagine that you find one of your favorite toys from childhood in a battered box high up in the closet. What would it be?

It would be wonderful to find ______________________________

because ____.

Toys were our treasures. Ten years ago you probably would have been able to remember more about your childhood and your toys than you can now. Ten years from now, even fewer clear memories will remain. First the toys disappear and then, slowly, the memories. Take your time. Preserve everything that you can now. Anything you write down will not vanish.

I remember a few of my old toys very vividly. I'm going to spread them out in one room and just look at them.

> It is the summer of my eighth year. Ike is president. I am in the bare upstairs living room on Devonshire. I have brought my army men, my Halloween dagger, and my baseball cards into this room and I sit with them all around me. It is bright outside. My parents are downstairs. I take my cards out and sort them into teams. I look

at my favorite ballplayers: Stan Musial, Red Schoendienst, Mickey Mantle. *My Weekly Reader* at school showed a picture of a boy in Michigan who was supposed to have more baseball cards than anyone in the United States. I went home and counted mine. I have two hundred more than he does. There are well over a thousand, including doubles, spread around me. I set them up in a team, with my favorite player at each position. I read the backs of some of them. I look at my Lone Ranger cards. I look at my Who's Who cards. I empty out my shoe box of army men and pick up the little green sniper with the high-powered rifle. I love this little guy.

For some reason I can see that little army man more clearly than anything else. He is made of hard, green rubber, sits in a crouch and squints through a telescopic sight. He is powerful. I can feel his exact size and shape in my fingers.

There are two joys in remembering childhood: first, in recognizing that we have not really changed at all; second, in seeing that we have, fortunately, changed so much. Holding my little marine (that's what he was!) I feel the same delight, and thus the long-ago past is not lost to me. The army men vanished, but not the child who delighted in them.

Your turn. Decide in which room you want to spread out your toys. Then do whatever you want. You're a kid—you get to play. Maybe you want to invite a friend over, or play with your brother or sister. Have fun. Be good.

Playing with My Old Toys

This year is ____________ . The president is ____________________________

__________________ . The room I am in is ______________________________

____ . The toys I have around me are

____

____

________________ . Outside the weather is ____________

____________________ . The first toy I pick up is my ______

_______________________ . I look at it carefully. I see ____

____

____

___________ . The next toy I pick up is _______________

________________ . Holding it, I feel ______________

____

__________________________ . Now, what I decide to do is

____

____

_____________________ . (Continue playing with your favorite toys.) ____________________________________

____

____

·7· THE WINDOWS OF CHILDHOOD

I am looking out the window of my bedroom, upstairs in the back of the house. I look across the backyard toward the treehouse and the creek lined with cement blocks, and then further toward the big family's house. They have eleven kids.

Now I turn and look out the other window. I see Eddie Nash's big yellow house, then the slopes up to the other houses, then the house where my beloved baby-sitter lives. I go across the hall into the living room and look across the street. That is where the doctor lives with his old, strange mother. She wants to teach me how to play the piano, but being alone with her scares the daylights out of me. I go downstairs and look out the kitchen window. I can see the creek better from here.

Looking out the windows of Home, you can begin to sketch in the surroundings. Little by little, you are completing a portrait of the world you grew up in.

Your task now is to look out every window you can remember. Do not hurry. Imagine putting your hands on the window sill. Then write down what you see, or hear. Next, look slowly to the right and left. Look at the sky and down at the ground. Memories will return.

LOOKING OUT THE WINDOWS

The first window I want to look out is ______________________

______________________ . The weather is ______________________

______________________. I see and/or hear ______________________

____.

____

______________________ . I also see ______________________

____

____

____ .

(Walk around the rooms at Home and look out the other windows.)

____

____

____

____

____

____

____

____

____

____

____

____

____

____

____

____

____ .

The best memory so far has been ______________________

because ____________________________________ .

I want to spend more time thinking about ______________

____ .

Now, and at any time in our journey, you may want to go back and add to your memories. Some travelers profit most from return voyages.

·8·
HOME EXACTLY THE WAY YOU REMEMBER IT

Now you are ready to re-create your Home. Look at the floor plans I drew of my Home on Devonshire. Using my memories from previous chapters, I included the location of furniture and the views from various windows. In addition, I noted a few places where important events occurred. I also laid out the backyard, the important trees, and the nearby surroundings.

Do the same thing with your Home. I have set aside two pages for you so you'll have lots of room to draw. Don't worry if your drawing isn't neat—you are the only one you have to please.

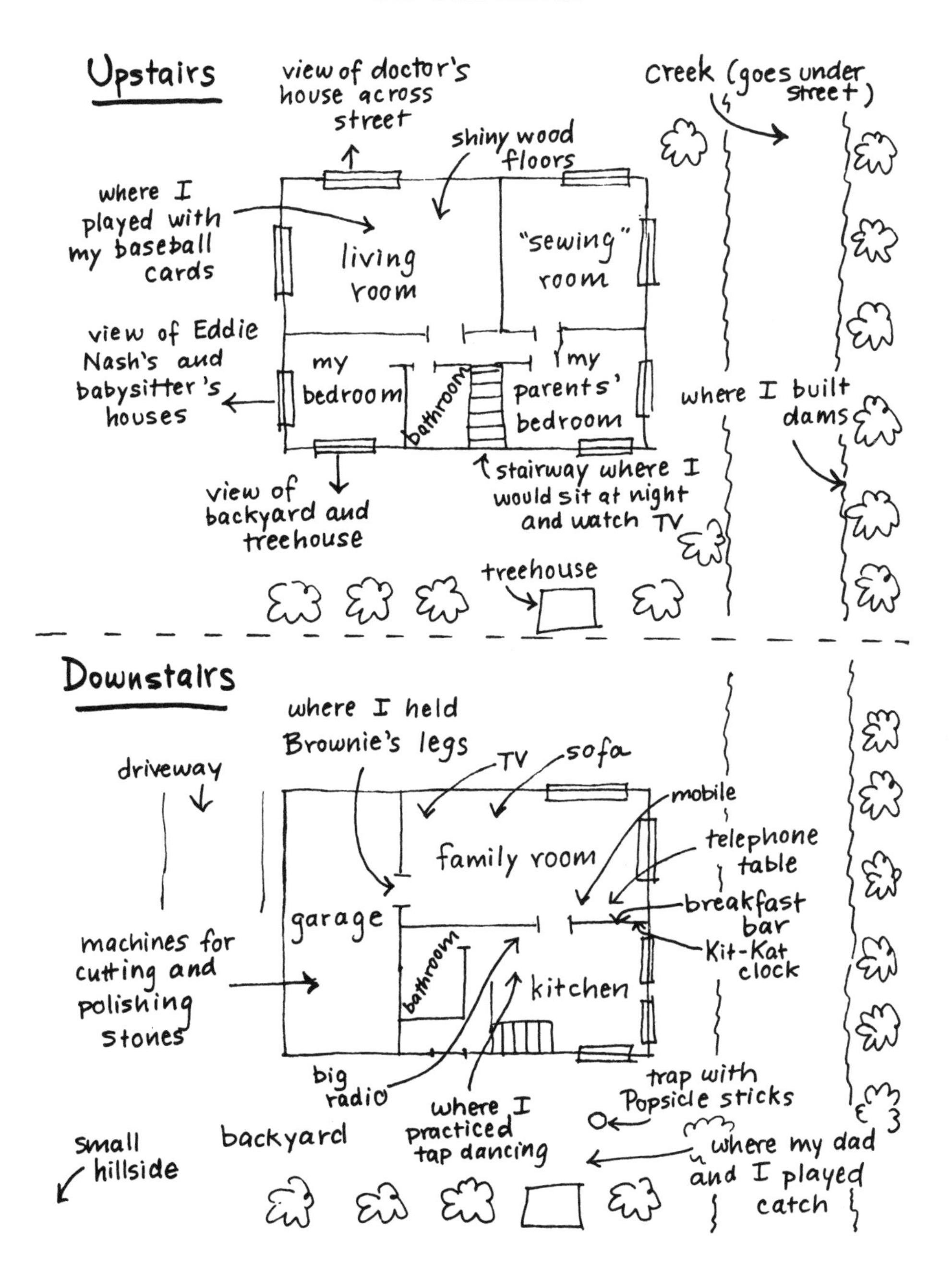
Upstairs
view of doctor's house across street
shiny wood floors
Creek (goes under street)
where I played with my baseball cards
living room
"sewing" room
view of Eddie Nash's and babysitter's houses
my bedroom
bathroom
my parents' bedroom
where I built dams
view of backyard and treehouse
stairway where I would sit at night and watch TV
treehouse
Downstairs
where I held Brownie's legs
TV
sofa
driveway
mobile
family room
telephone table
garage
breakfast bar
Kit-Kat clock
machines for cutting and polishing stones
bathroom
kitchen
big radio
trap with Popsicle sticks
where I practiced tap dancing
small hillside
backyard
where my dad and I played catch

A FLOOR PLAN OF MY OLD HOME

A Floor Plan of My Old Home

· 9 ·
WALKING THE NEIGHBORHOOD

I walk out the front door of my house and turn left up the street. There are no curbs. The street is gravel pressed into tar. On my side of the street I walk past Eddie Nash's big yellow-and-white house, then another house, then past my baby-sitter's house. He and his younger, jerky brother are out in the yard wrestling on an old mattress.

I cross the street and walk back toward my house. I walk past a field with buckeye trees. Then I walk past the doctor's house and down to the corner. Up the hill to my left is the market. Across the street is a huge lot full of weeds. The weeds are so tall they are like a jungle, full of trails and hideouts. I cross the street and walk past the house where the boy who played first base lives, and then down to the corner past the house where the dog that bit me lives. Then I turn right, past the house where the big family lives. They told me to walk in anytime without knocking.

On my left is a big park with an old railroad engine! I fell off it once and got a bloody earlobe. I throw some rocks at it. I cut across the block and walk back toward my house. There is a small bridge here across the creek and then a big, bare backyard. Now, I'm under the tree where my father built the treehouse. I climb up the ladder of boards nailed to the tree. It is the summer of 1954. I sit in my treehouse and wait to see what happens.

Take a walk around your neighborhood. Do what I did, but add even more details. Take your time. It's morning and lunch is a long way off.

Write down buildings, people, animals, cars, or any other details that catch your eye. (Adding cars to your experience might be an especially vivid way of re-creating the feel of a neighborhood. If I were going to do my exercise again, I would imagine autos parked in various places, none of them older than 1954. A world in which the latest model is a shiny, new '54 . . . now, that is a lost childhood!)

Reliving a Walk around the Old Neighborhood

I stand at my front door and see ______________________________.

I look to the right and see ______________________________.

To the left I see ______________________________.

The direction I head is ____________________. I see __________

______________________________.

(Continue with a long walk around your neighborhood:)

____

____

____

____

·10·
A Map of the World of Childhood

I'm going to sketch a simple map of the neighborhood I just walked through. Note that I add more details and fill in locations of other memories.

Carefully make a map of your own. As you try to fill in blank areas, the past will grow clearer.

My Old Neighborhood

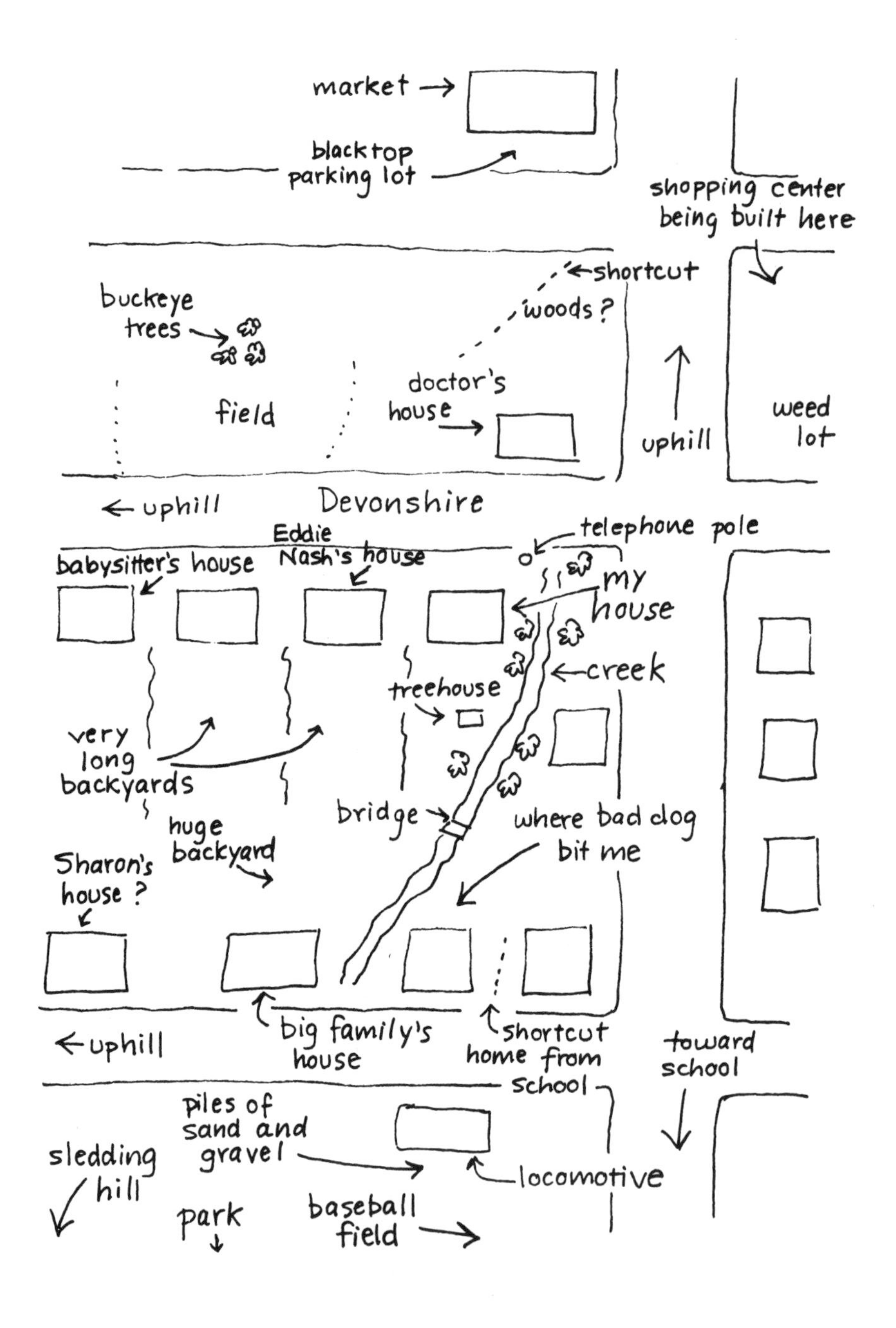

A Map of My Old Neighborhood

·11· The World of Play

Let's think about games, play, and everything we did in the days when we could do as we pleased. Here is a list of what I might have done on a summer's day when I was eight years old. Expand your list, as I have, whenever something interesting or insightful occurs to you.

1. Play catch with my father in the backyard
2. Go to baseball practice
3. Go swimming
4. Play army men down in the creek
5. Shoot my Wham-O slingshot (I had forgotten this!)
6. Play split or mumbly-peg with my pocketknife (now I can remember a lot of the stages of mumbly-peg)
7. Have a spear fight with tall, uprooted weeds
8. Go to the store for a Popsicle
9. Form a club—that's it! Now I remember how my baby-sitter's brother was always forming clubs and charging dues. Then the club would fold, and he kept the money. That's why he was a jerk! Once he held a "white elephant sale" and sold a bunch of stuff in sealed brown paper bags for

ten cents a bag. Nearly everything was junk, but one bag contained his famous World War II gas mask, and that was the come-on.

10. Pick buckeyes
11. Tease Eddie Nash about his glasses (he was a crybaby)
12. Go for a bike ride
13. Wrestle on the gravel piles in the park
14. Play guns (the game of choice)
15. Play flips (a gambling game in which you could lose your entire collection of baseball cards in a feverish afternoon)
16. Sell Kool-Aid (I did this once)
17. Box with somebody
18. Take batting practice with the red ball on the string hanging from the garage door
19. Watch TV (there was only one channel. This was only in case there was absolutely nothing else to do.)
20. Climb trees
21. Have a fight with water guns
22. Play Monopoly or some other board game (Chutes and Ladders, Clue)
23. Ditch somebody

Now make your list of activities.

A List of What I Did When I Could Do as I Pleased

____

____

____

Even though we will spend the second half of this book searching for Wisdom, this is a good opportunity to stop for a moment to see what we can learn about ourselves. Play, when it is really fun, is not play. The imaginary activity becomes real. We criticize our playmates for "not playing right," and we mean they are doing something that breaks the illusion of reality. We want, in play, to become a person we could not possibly be otherwise. Play is the arena for a version of ourselves that, when we grow up, we have to conceal, or find an outlet for in the world of work and responsibility.

For example, when I look at the last list I made, I see many examples of a delight in power and in the humiliation of rivals. I was the winner who loved to rub it in and the loser who argued hotly that he had not really lost. I might lose at a game of Monopoly, but I would find a way to win the argument afterward. Now the question is, When did I stop acting this way (because this kind of behavior is not easily tolerated among adults)? or How did I find a way to play the same games without others knowing it? It occurs to me now that what I have done as an adult is to create imaginary opponents. As a writer I often feel myself in an unconscious race with college friends from twenty years ago. I write books not just to write books, but to beat others at a game they don't know is being played.

Look at your list of games and favorite activities and see what you can learn about yourself. What kind of child do you see? Are there common emotions that run through many of the games? What kind of person were you pretending to be? Themes you can look for might involve: power; fear; community; cunning; greed; fantasy of a particular kind; feeling like an outsider, a leader, or a follower; being a creator of harmony or discord; delighting in sharing or deceiving.

After looking carefully at my list, I see a child who ____________________

____

____.

My favorite game really seemed to be about ______________________________

____

____.

In play I loved to feel ____

____

____.

Here is a difficult question. You have already answered a version of this once, but now try to go deeper: What are the similarities and differences between yourself as a child at play and yourself as an adult?

Thinking hard about this, I would say the similarities I see are ________

____

____

____.

The differences I see are ____

____

____

____.

Is there any way in which you have carried the games and passions of childhood into maturity?

I believe ____

____

____

____

____.

Based upon what you now see about yourself as a child and as an adult, give yourself some good advice.

The wisest advice I have is ______________________________

____

____

____.

In this way, you begin to chart your future—something you'll do more of later on.

· 12 ·
MORE MEMORY LOCATIONS

Let's return once more to childhood and see if we can add a few more pieces to the puzzle. Look again at the map you drew of your old neighborhood. In this chapter we want to add memory locations to our maps.

When I look at the map of my old neighborhood and wonder what happened in the blank areas, images return from the past. I remember a teenager on a motorcycle who challenged me to a race when I was on my bike climbing up the long hill to the store. Riding my bike on the other hill, I coasted down with no hands, showing off for my father. Then he told me to try to pedal, and I couldn't keep my balance. Starting at my map and wondering what happened to me at various places, more memories return. (Note: I'm continuing the numbered list from the previous chapter.)

24. Scooter race
25. No-hands bike ride
26. Where the dog bit me
27. Where my mom comforted me in her arms after the dog had bitten me, and the lady who owned the dog came and looked at me
28. Some kids in a club with a flag (the Reindeer Club?)
29. A tall tree I climbed to the top of, frightening my mom

30. A shortcut home from school
31. Where I put nails under Eddie's father's car
32. Where I waited for the bus to camp
33. A sledding hill in the winter (I just remembered another toy—a great sled, better than anyone else's.)
34. A little foot trap I dug and covered with Popsicle sticks (My mother told me it was too dangerous.)
35. The only time I ever hit a bird with a stone

Look at the map of your old neighborhood again. You spent countless hours playing and having adventures there. Look at each area carefully, and make a list of what happened where. Add the details from this and the previous chapter's list to your map, and you will have a remarkably complete image of the world you wandered through long ago.

Other Events in My Neighborhood

____

____

____

____

____

____

____

____

· 13 ·
SCHOOL

So far we have worked outward from the rooms at Home, to a floor plan of Home, to a map of our neighborhoods with numerous memory locations. Now we turn to school.

As we did in previous chapters, we will make lists of memories and then make maps. Your list can contain anything that has to do with your school experience: games, the names of classmates or teachers, pictures on the classroom wall, toys, books, displays, wonderful or terrible experiences, secret places, locations where you felt strong emotions, playground equipment, objects or displays that fascinated you in the classroom, places you remember in the neighborhood surrounding the schoolyard.

I have far more memories of the schoolyard than of the inside of the school building. Here is my list in the order that the memories returned to me:

1. A bully named Tommy Bus holding me in a headlock in the corner of the playground
2. Playing "space cadets" with a kitchen knife from home
3. Playing kickball
4. The corner of the schoolyard where we played "prisoners"
5. Throwing ice balls against the brick wall of the gym

6. Running down the blacktop ramp
7. Drawing war pictures in class
8. Making "money" with the classroom paper cutter
9. Studying the Amazon, the anaconda, the tapir, and Indians who built huts from palm fronds; the word *manioc* (?)
10. The candy store across the street, where we bought Sen-Sen and yard-long penny ropes of licorice
11. Some kid we called "Nature Boy" because he pointed out the difference between the way sparrows and robins fly

Make your list.

I remember ____

____

____

____

____

____

____

____

____

____

____

The next task is map making. I have included the school and the schoolyard on the same map because I have so few memories of the former. I have set aside two pages for you.

Making these diagrams not only provides a location for our memories but also helps us recall forgotten experiences. When you finish, look at each part of your map. Try to fill in the blank areas. You spent hours and hours in school and running around the playground; be patient and you will have the pleasure of discovering hidden memories.

Circled numbers refer to items on my list.

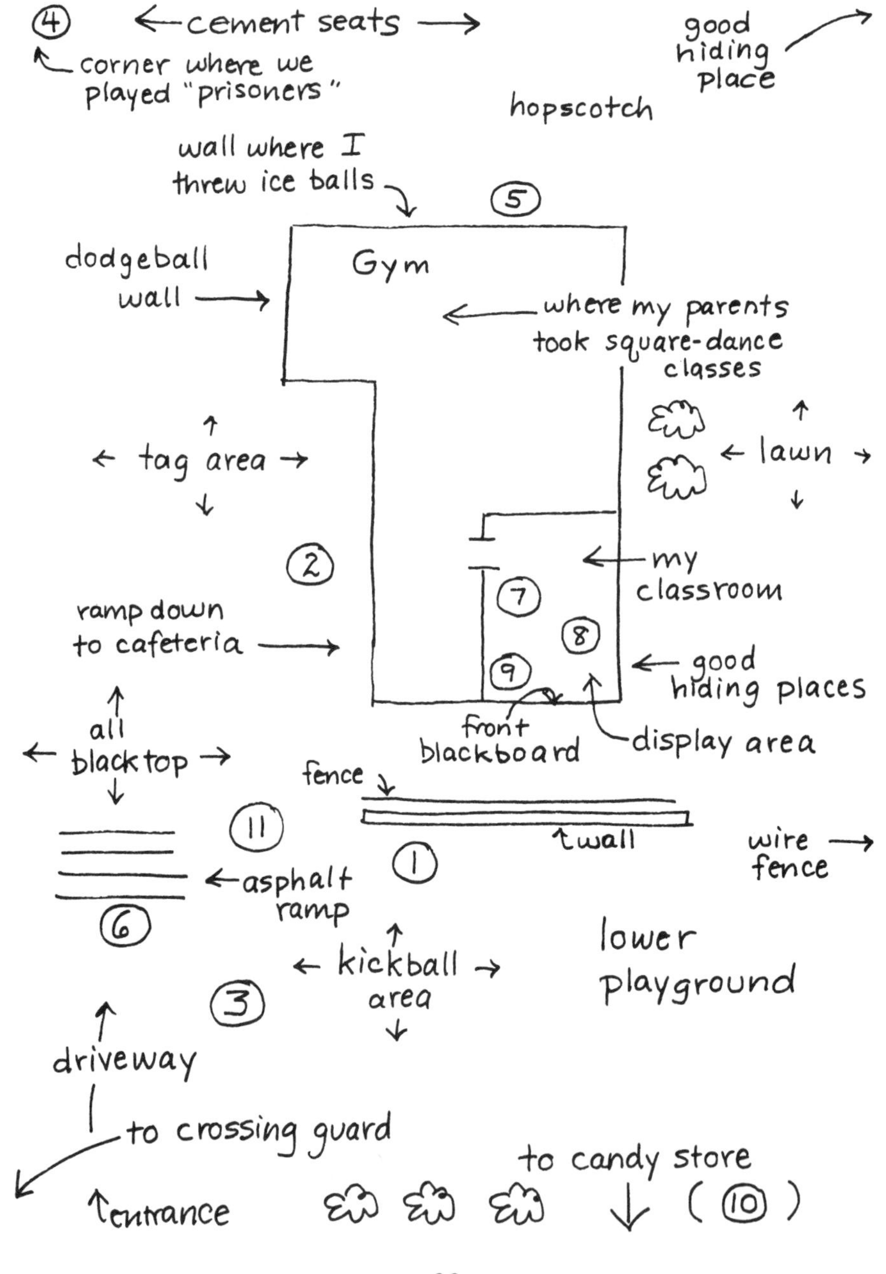

Floor Plan of My Classroom with Important Memory Locations

Map of My Schoolyard with Important Memory Locations

·14·
SILENT REVERIE

We have already tried several ways to relive childhood, and in the next section I will suggest a few more. Now, however, we are ready for the simplest: Look at your maps and daydream.

Go back to all the places and simply reexperience what you did and how you felt. There is something healing and delightful in dreaming over the past. Your separate memories are woven together on the previous pages. You can move from one to another and link them all in sweet, silent reverie.

We forget we were young. We forget the world that meant everything to us. We forget the people who meant so much to us and the games that were so fascinating. In this book we re-member, we put ourselves back together.

In recording your reverie, just write and don't worry where the sentence is going. Let one memory, emotion, or image lead to another. Whenever you are stuck, do one of three things: Look back through this book; or start a sentence with "I remember when . . . "; or, just keep adding "and . . . " without worrying about punctuation.

Here is my reverie (unedited, as all my samples are on this journey).

> I start in a headlock with Tommy Bus and he is threatening me with something, and now I see Nature Boy's face. He looks something like Knucklehead Smith, a puppet I remember from TV. And

now I see the skipping way the sparrow flies and am amazed that Nature Boy notices such things, and now I remember that he brings bird's eggs and nests to school. We teased him with a toothpaste jingle from TV because he had buckteeth: "Bucky, Bucky Beaver . . . use the new Ipana . . . it's dandy for your teeth!" Now, I can hear the splat of ice balls against the gym wall, and now we are getting in trouble about it. Ice balls are dangerous, the principal warns.

Now I am at home playing with my baseball cards and I have just given away my two favorite players, Stan Musial and Red Schoendienst, and feel like a fool. Now I am downstairs crying because the old lady across the street wants to teach me how to play the piano and she moves so slowly that she terrifies me. And I tell my mother, "I knew I would have bad luck because I threw snake eyes today in Monopoly." And my father has to go across the street and tell the old woman I don't want piano lessons. Now the doctor is giving me a shot, he makes house calls. And now I am riding no-hands down the hill and am amazed and then disappointed because my dad isn't impressed.

I could have gone on like this for a long time, but my entries are only to help you create yours. I took a stream-of-consciousness approach to my reverie; you can do the same, or make more lists, or write a letter to yourself, or focus on one part of your childhood, or let everything flow together. The only rule is: Do what brings you pleasure.

A Reverie on Childhood

Now we seek Wisdom once more. Let me fire some questions at you about your childhood. Write your answers quickly and see if you can surprise yourself with insights.

Who were you as a child?

I was a child who ______________________________

____.

Tell me more.

I was also a child who ______________________________

____.

What was important to you?

Most important to me was ______________________________

____.

What were your strongest emotions?

I remember feeling ______________________________

____.

How did you feel about yourself?

I felt ______________________________

____

____.

When were you the happiest?

I was happiest when ______________________________

______________________________.

When were you the saddest?

I was the saddest when ______________________________

______________________________.

Give a long, thoughtful answer to this: What image of yourself is beginning to emerge?

Looking back, I see a child who ______________________________

____

____

____

____

____

____

____

____

______________________________.

These last two pages provide a good transition to the Inner World of Childhood, where we will look more carefully beneath the surface of the childhood we have just re-created.

Remember, we are not looking for dark secrets. In fact, this journey is constructed on the notion that most childhoods do not contain dark and terrible secrets. We simply want to learn more about our personalities as children in order to see ourselves as adults more clearly. Then we can use this self-knowledge to find the most fruitful paths into the future.

PART • 2

THE INNER WORLD OF CHILDHOOD

·15· MEMORY PHOTOGRAPHS

In the first part of our journey, we put together a collection of memories of a specific time and place from the past. For the pleasure of it, we have crossed the boundary several times between remembering and reliving. We have occasionally used our childhood experiences as a springboard for reflection about our adult life. In the second half of our journey, we will do this much more often as we turn from the physical landscape of childhood to the emotional. We have a map of our neighborhoods; now we want a map of our psyches.

We are going to turn inward. We have talked about activities. Now we want to talk more about how we felt doing these activities. On the next page, I have created a collection of "memory photographs." These could never be in a photo album, because they all come from my mind. They are the pictures I wish I had. Looking at them all together, I can begin to get an overview of my emotional life as a child.

Creating this collection was simple. I started with a vivid memory. For example, in the first photo I used words and arrows to re-create the image I have in memory of being in the top of a tree behind our house. My memory includes images of my mother, myself, the tree, a creek below the tree, and houses in the background. I added these to the picture with arrows showing where they would appear if I had a photograph of that memory. The only subtle point is this: *The words and arrows I have used are not to help me see the photo on the page more clearly, but to help me see my inner image more clearly*. By setting up the memory as a photo on the page and locating its essential details within the frame, the memory itself becomes more vivid.

The final task is to add a title to each photo. My titles are about my feelings or emotional experiences, because these are what I want to explore.

Look at my collection of memory photos and then create your own. Start with an image of a vivid memory in your mind and then imagine how it would appear as a photo. Add clarifying details to this memory image by adding words and arrows on the page. Finish by giving the photo a title that refers to your feelings as a child. Let the memories return in any order.

What stuns me about my personal collection of memory photographs is that they show me generally happy as a child. I had always thought I had an unhappy early childhood. The unhappiness, I realize now for the first time, did not start until after I left the house on Devonshire. Only the last picture, when my father tells me about the divorce, is sad.

Is there anything that strikes you immediately about your collection of memory photographs?

What I notice first is ______________________________________

____

____

____

____

____

____.

MEMORY PHOTOGRAPHS

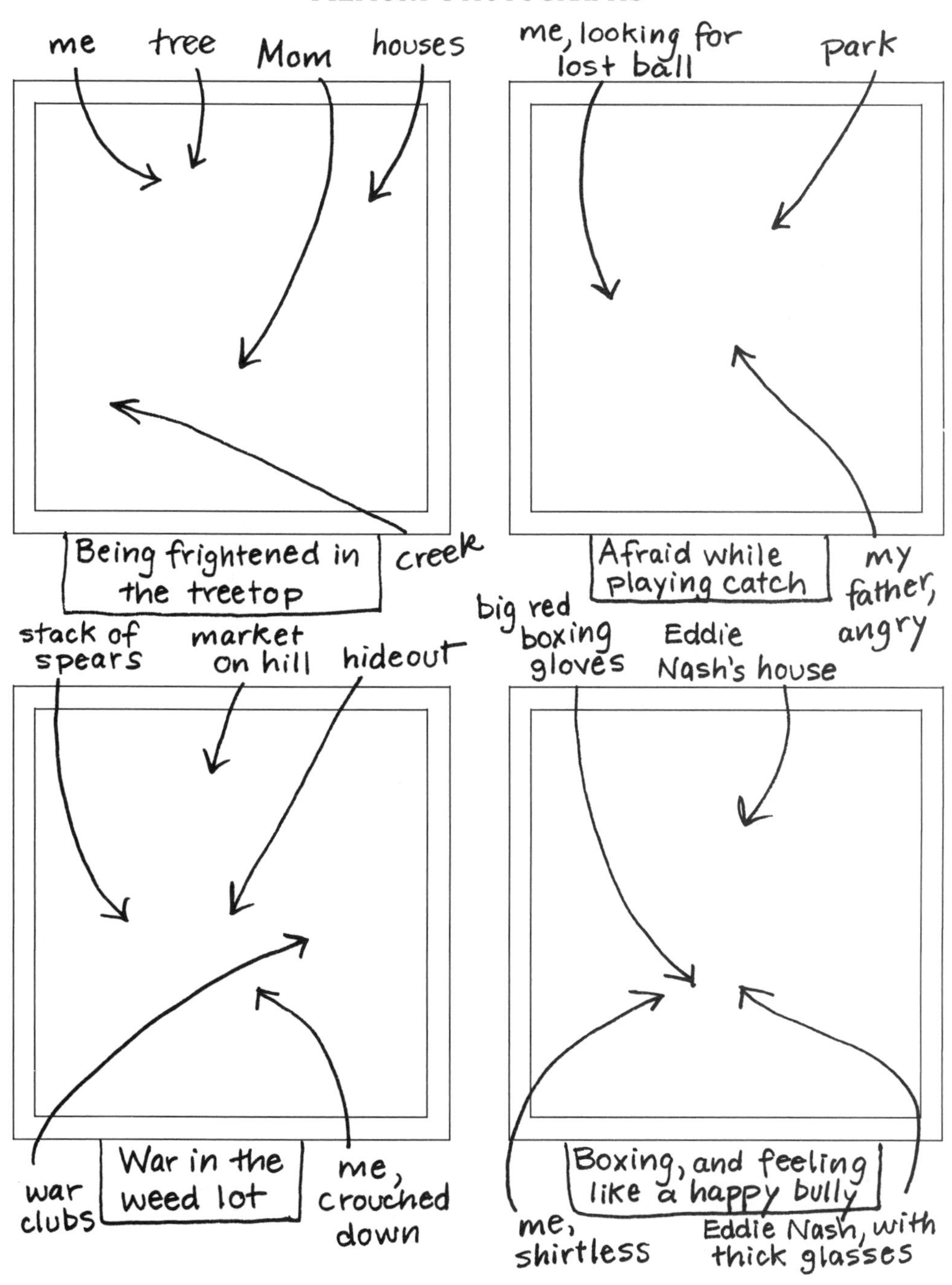

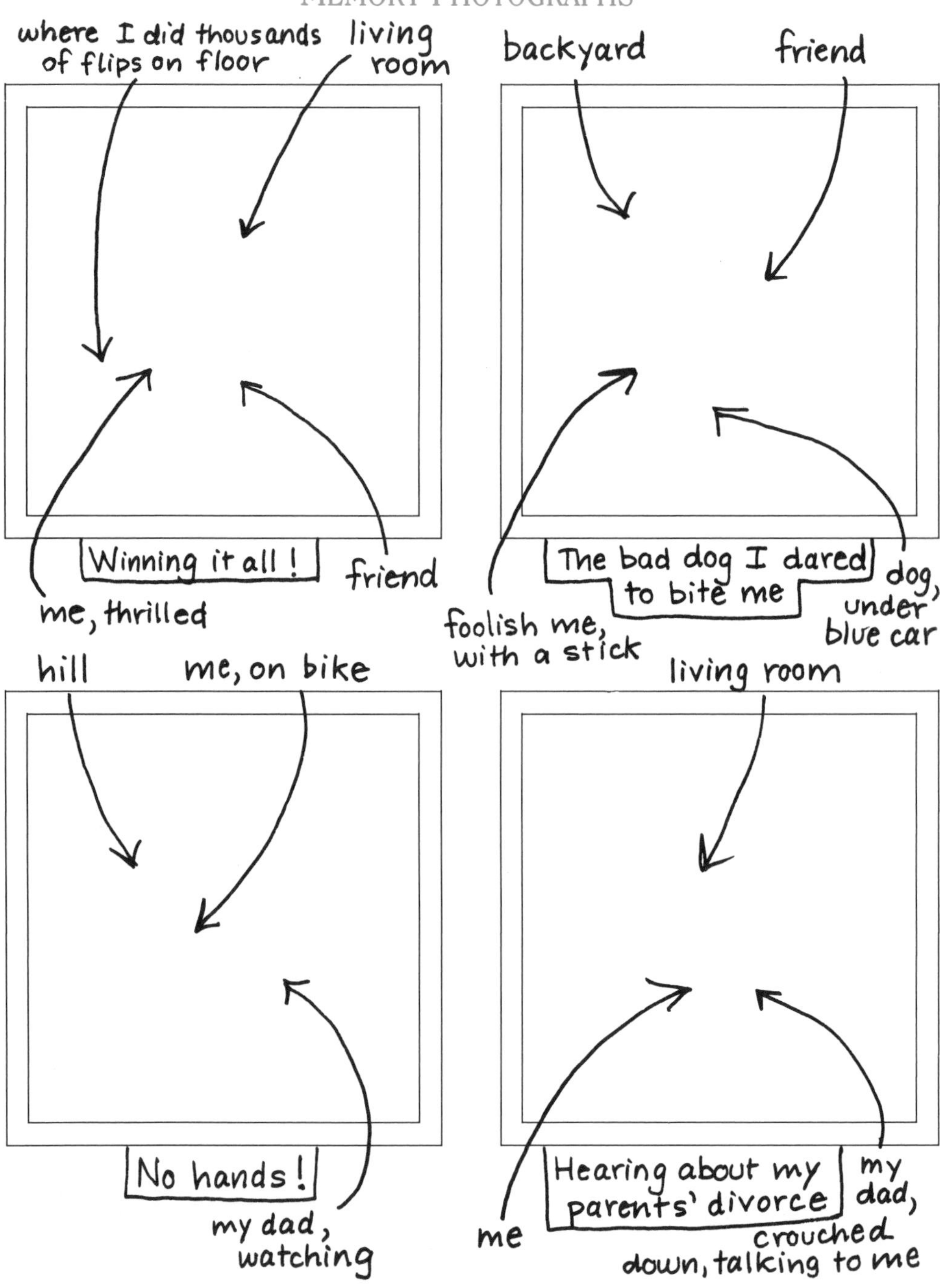
where I did thousands of flips on floor
living room
Winning it all!
me, thrilled
friend
backyard
friend
The bad dog I dared to bite me
foolish me, with a stick
dog, under blue car
hill
me, on bike
No hands!
my dad, watching
living room
Hearing about my parents' divorce
me
my dad, crouched down, talking to me

Your Memory Photographs

Most of my feelings in the photos are typically boyish. I don't feel uncomfortable about them now. There is aggression and delight in power, and a kind of boyish meanness. But I feel good about this kid. Like many teenagers, I had some dark adolescent years, but I can find no source for this in 1954. I was normal. What a strange delight!

What I feel about myself as a child is ______________________________

____

____

________________ . I seem to have been someone who ________________

____

____

____

____

________________________________ . When I look for seeds of my present

personality in who I was then, I see __________________________________

____

____ .

I recognize one seed of my present personality in those baseball cards. They were like a world I could manipulate, control, and rearrange. My toy soldiers gave me the same feeling of looking down on a small world. That feeling led me, as an adult, to writing books (like this one) in which I set up little worlds and rearrange them. Instead of shuffling teams, I shuffle chapters. It gives me the same feeling of delight.

Looking as carefully and deeply as I can at the child in my photos, I see

____

____

____

____

____

____

____

____

____

____

____

____

____

____.

·16·
LIFE WITH PARENTS

In this chapter we try to see the inner character of the adults we lived with when we were children. For the sake of simplicity, I will assume you grew up at Home with both your mother and father present; if this is not the case, change the tasks in this chapter to make them relevant. For example, if your grandmother raised you, change the questions about "mother" to "grandmother" and delete the tasks about "father." If you were raised by your aunt and uncle, change "mother" to "aunt" and "father" to "uncle," and so forth.

Knowing more about who our parents were long ago, we learn more about our own past and present. We can often find interesting clues to our parents' personalities by thinking about their lives before we were born. I have a tendency to think of my father as if he were no one but my father, as if he were born with no other destiny or interest in life. It is also difficult for me to think of my mother as a woman with her own life outside of, and independent of, mine.

It always struck me that they both had an unusual attitude toward money. My father often got angry when I would wad up dollar bills and put them in my front pocket instead of placing them neatly in my wallet. Money was also precious to my mother in ways I could not understand; not just important but *precious.* This becomes understandable when I reflect that they both came to adulthood in the Depression. When my father finally found work in the 1930s, his family was down to its last fifty dollars. My mother arrived in Los Angeles in the late 1930s, knowing no one and with twenty-five cents in her purse. Of course money was precious. Of course you didn't wad it up and carelessly shove the wondrous stuff in your pocket.

Tell me about your parents. What do you know about their lives before you were born? What were the major experiences they went through growing up?

When I think of my father's life before I was born, I see a man who

____

____

____

_______________________________________ .

Some of the most important experiences in his early life were __________

____

____

____

____

_______________________________________ .

When I think about whether any of these things explain aspects of his personality, I find that ______________________________

____

When I think of my mother's life before I was born, I see a woman who

Some of the most important experiences in her early life were

When I consider whether any of these things explain aspects of her personality, I find that

Now, think about your father at Home during the childhood you have been exploring. What memories do you have of him that you have not already recorded?

I see him

Here is a blunt question that might lead to Wisdom: What kind of father was he?

He was the kind of father who

Follow the same pattern with your mother. First talk about the memories you have of her at Home and then try to state, as clearly as possible, what kind of mother she was.

When I think of my mother, I see her ______________________________

____

____

____

____.

She was the kind of mother who ______________________________

____

____

____.

Here is another simple but fertile question: What were the similarities and differences between them?

When I try to think of the similarities between my parents, I see ______

____

____

____

When I try to think of the differences I see

Remember, if you find something especially worth remembering, something that is Wisdom—put a star beside it.

Now we are both about to attempt a challenging feat of memory and imagination. We will return to childhood and "interview" our parents.

If you could return to your Home and find your parents just as they were long ago, what questions would you have for them? And what could you learn from that remarkable encounter?

I would ask my parents

I would be trying to learn ______________________________________

____

____.

Here is my own attempt. First I established a specific scene, then I entered it and asked my father a series of questions. This is not as difficult as it may seem. Whenever you played dolls or cowboys as a child, you created a scene and then let it come to life. Often you played several roles. Do the same thing now in a quest for Wisdom.

In 1954 my dad was 48 and I think my mom was 42. There are a lot of things I need to ask both of them. I'll set it up this way:

Time: Summer 1954
Place: St. Louis
Weather: Hot, cloudless, humid
Location: The family room downstairs in the house on Devonshire
Situation: My father is sitting on the couch and I sit across from him. The black fan is on, blowing back and forth between us. For some reason it does not seem at all strange that I, as an adult, am talking to him while I, as a child, am also outside playing.

Q. [I am speaking] Tell me about your life now.

A. I work at Carradine Hat Factory. I do an honest day's work for an honest day's pay. That is what I owe the company. I got out of the Navy eight years ago. I work hard, but that's the way life is.

Q. Tell me about your boy.

A. Biff is a good boy, but he is a bit of a scaredy-cat. I'd like him to be better at baseball. It aggravates me that he is so afraid when he is batting. But he is a good boy. I love him.

Q. Tell me about your wife.

A. Marion is a strange woman. I never knew anyone like her. She has a strange power. I don't know if you would call it psychic or what. She is also very creative. I wish she got along better with my mother.

Q. What do you want for your son?

A. I want him to be a man—tough, hard working, less nonsense, proud, unafraid. I don't care what he grows up to be, I just want him to be the best he can be at that particular thing.

(Biff, myself as a child, comes in and sits next to my father. I am surprised to see how short and small-boned he is. But he also looks all boy: no shirt; dirty jeans; black, high-top tennis shoes; a Marty Marion baseball glove on his hand. Now I, as an adult, talk to myself as a child.)

Q. What do you want to be, young man?

A. A pitcher for the New York Yankees or president of the U.S.A.

(I continue my conversation with the two of them. My mother comes in later and I talk to her as well.)

Here is a list of questions you might ask your parents and yourself as a child. Call in brothers, sisters, or other relatives if you wish. It's your world. Everyone you talk to will speak the truth and no one will be hurt. You all seek Wisdom together.

Circle the questions that are interesting to you and then work them into your interview wherever you please.

1. How would you describe yourself?

2. What are your goals? (Pay attention to how your parents may answer this differently.)
3. How do you feel about your spouse?
4. What are the happiest days in your life now? Ever?
5. What are the most difficult now? Ever?
6. How would you describe your child?
7. What are your child's strengths and weaknesses?
8. What are your main worries?
9. What are your strengths and weaknesses?
10. How would you define a good husband/wife?
11. What do you and your spouse quarrel about?
12. What have you tried to teach your child?
13. How has your child changed you?
14. What is your goal in life?

You are looking for several kinds of Wisdom in this interview. You want to see the inner character of each of your parents more clearly. You want to see who you were inside, long ago. And you want to find the ideas and values that shaped your childhood, the good and bad lessons you learned from your parents. You will probably want to include in the interview anyone who touched your life at Home. Usher them into the room whenever you please.

An Interview with My Parents (and Others)

Year and Season: ______________________

Place: ______________________

Weather: ______________________

Location:

Situation:

·17· A Family Portrait

Let's make one more memory picture together: the perfect family portrait. Think of your mother and father and yourself, not as your would have dressed to have your picture taken in a portrait studio, but as you would have looked on a normal day in your childhood. Imagine each family member holding an object that is important to him or her, something that seems to symbolize that person's essence.

I imagine my father in his gray work clothes, holding a black lunch bucket. He always seemed to me the archetypal working man. My mother would be wearing slacks, a blouse, and her fancy eyeglasses. She would be holding a dapping stick (a stone-polishing tool). Her passion was arts and crafts. I would be standing in front of them in my cowboy shirt, jeans, and black high-tops and holding a wooden Halloween dagger that they had made for me.

When I think about this imaginary portrait of each of us in our most characteristic appearance, I see three people who were in separate worlds. My father and mother, in my imaginary picture, have no more in common than they did in real life. As I write this, I realize that this insight has never struck me before with exactly this force. When I look at myself as a child, I see a boy who really had no idea how different his parents were and who rarely thought about them except in terms of himself. This also surprises me and is worth a star of Wisdom.

Notice that I have used words and arrows to create my family portrait, using the same technique we used for the memory photographs. Do the same thing yourself, and then we will talk about the portrait you have created. First, tell me briefly about the photo you will construct.

I will start with myself. The important object I would be holding is ____

____

____

____.

I would be wearing ______________________________

____

____

____.

My father's most characteristic clothes would be ______________

____

____

____.

The object he would be holding that would represent his personality would be

____

____

____.

My mother's most characteristic clothes would be _______________

____

____

____

____.

I imagine her holding _________________________

____

____.

Now fill in your family portrait with details about the background, the important objects, and the clothing. Describe the expression on each person's face. Include brothers, sisters, or other family members if you wish. You are making a portrait that will help you see the essential character of yourself as a child and each important person in your life.

Portrait of the Biffle Family, 1954

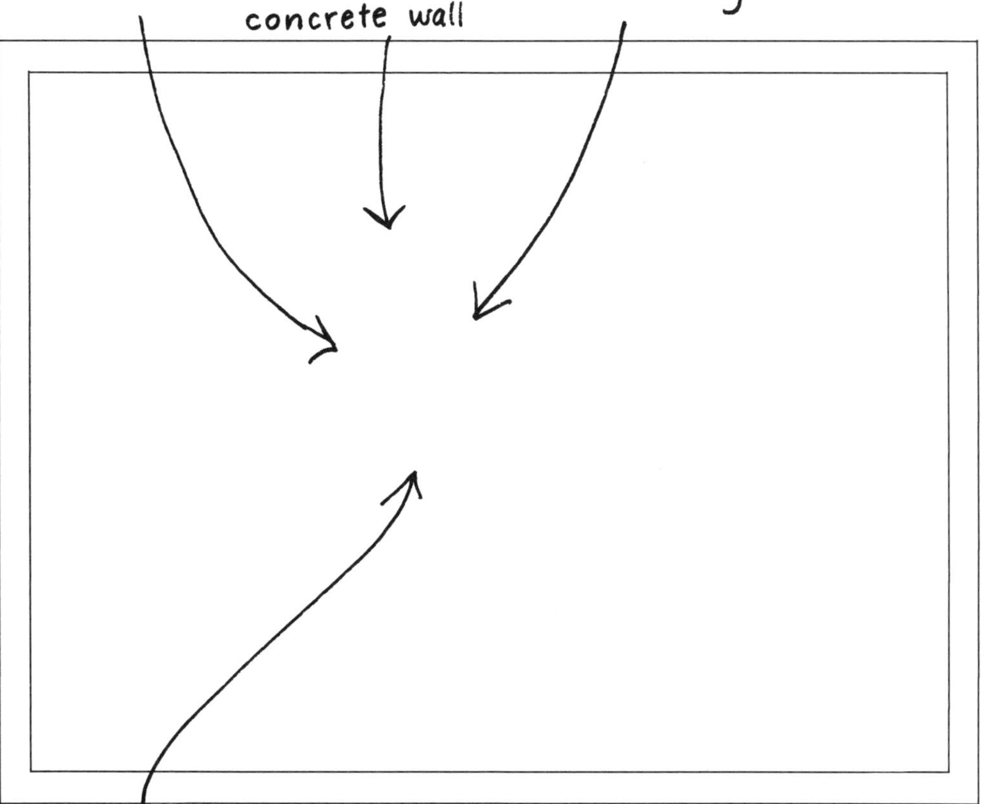

PORTRAIT OF THE ______________________ FAMILY, ______

·18·
A Wisdom Meditation

Our next step is to think as deeply as we can about each person in our family portrait. We want to understand as much as possible about their inner character, their true strengths and weaknesses.

This is the slowest I have written any part of this book. I am looking at my family portrait as carefully as I can.

I will begin with my father.

> When I look at my father standing there in his work clothes, I see a man who was never lazy, in any memory I have of him. And he was never exuberant. I cannot imagine my father whooping for joy, even if the Cardinals won the World Series, or Rocky Marciano knocked somebody out in the first round. No part of his character was lazy or passionately exuberant or capable of complaint. His life was hard and he never whined.
>
> Inside him I see something tough, hard, and cranky. He was easy to irritate.
>
> (I'm writing very slowly now and crossing out every other sentence.) I see love in him. Yes, but what kind? A strange, meek love with my mother. He followed her in her passions. She was the font of ideas and direction in the marriage. He polished stones for her

jewelry. He cut the designs she drew into wood. He followed her into square dancing. When he wouldn't follow her to California, the marriage ended.

He loved me, but with a nervous, arm's-distance love. He believed the embrace of love would make me soft. His greatest weakness, with me at least, was lack of gentleness. He lacked, in those years, understanding and empathy. He never saw that I lived in one world and he lived in another.

Now I look at my mother. Creative. She could do anything with her hands—draw, paint, make mosaics, embroider. She made the most beautiful silver jewelry I have ever seen. Much more than empathetic, she was psychic. She knew my insides. My father didn't. That was it—that was why I was so much closer to her. She knew how I felt. My father always wanted me to feel something else, something more manly. My mother knew precisely how to delight me. My father had no clue. (I never saw that before.) She drew my wonderful dagger for Halloween on a piece of plywood and my father cut it out. She painted it silver, with red on the blade for blood. The blood was the perfect, boy-delighting touch.

Also, inside her I see determination and ambition. After the divorce she went back to college at 40, before women were doing that. She finished three years in two and was Phi Beta Kappa. But what was her weakness? She made everyone into her audience.

And now the skinny little boy. What do I see inside him? I am looking as hard and as honestly as I can. He fears his father. He is totally enchanted by his mother. She is the most wondrous creature ever born. She can do anything. I see happiness in him, unreflective contentment. He knows he will never grow up. Time is long.

He is competitive. He has no close friends. (I never saw that before.) He is a rotten friend. He wants to win and has no interest in the arts of teamwork or cooperation. If he can't stand out from a group, he doesn't want to be part of it. Most of his games have large measures of fantasized violence, typical of a normal American boy in the 1950s.

What I like about this boy is his passion and his silliness. His greatest weakness is that he has no deep feeling for anyone but his mother.

Before you try this Wisdom meditation on your family portrait, let's think again about the definition of *Wisdom.* I said Wisdom was anything worth remembering, and that is certainly true. Plato, the philosopher I have spent most of my adult life explaining to undergraduates, would agree.

In the "Allegory of the Cave," Plato describes a group of prisoners chained in a cave who have spent their lives looking at the shadows on the cave wall. Unknown to them a fire is tended behind them by men who walk back and forth in front of the flame holding wooden objects whose images are cast on the wall. The prisoners think the shadows are reality.

When one of the prisoners is released and led out of the cave, he is stunned. He encounters the real world of sunlight, trees, lakes, and fields. When he was chained in the cave, he accepted without questioning that the shadows were the only reality. Outside the cave, he not only discovers a new world, but also sees that the universe contains both truth and illusion. He has gained Wisdom.

Wisdom is what you find after you begin to question your most comfortable beliefs. In this book you have been trying to tell truth from illusion, shadow from reality. Now you are ready to try as hard as you can to pierce through any false images you have of yourself, your parents, and any other people in your family portrait.

Use any of these four questions to help you see each person as clearly as possible.

1. What strengths and weaknesses do you see in each person in your family portrait? (Everyone has both. Guard against any tendency you may have to be too kind or too harsh.)

2. What similarities and differences do you see between any two people in your family portrait? (All people are alike in some ways and utterly individual in other ways. If we could truly describe the similarities and differences between two personalities, we would probably arrive at a perfect description of each.)
3. If you were not involved in this family, how would you see each of these people? (The more fully you answer this question, the more objective your portrait will be.)
4. What was your relationship with ______________________ really like? (Think slowly and carefully about what was really happening between yourself and each family member in the portrait. Remember that your side of the relationship is important, but it is only half of what you want to understand.)

You are turning away from illusion and the shadows on the cave wall. You are seeking the clear, bright world of fact. Go slowly. (It took me an entire morning to write the description at the start of this chapter.) Review each observation you make to be sure it fits the person you are describing.

My Wisdom Meditation on My Family Portrait

____

____

____

____

____

____

Creating your family portrait has helped you understand yourself and your parents as you were long ago. Now that Wisdom can help you gain insight into your present personality. Let us try dividing your present personality into three kinds of characteristics: those you share with your mother, those you share with your father, and those that are uniquely your own.

Some similarities between my father and myself are: ____________

____

____

____________.

Some similarities between my mother and myself are: ____________

____

____

____ .

Some traits I don't seem to share with either of them are: ____________

____

____

____ .

Some unique features of your personality may simply be related to the fact that you grew up at a different time than your parents and were part of a different generation. For example, I noted earlier the difference between myself and my parents in our attitudes toward money. I was a child who grew up in the 1960s. I was part of an affluent generation; my friends burned money in the streets of San Francisco.

My parents grew up when __________________________

____ .

So their values were ______________________________

____

____

__________________________________ . I, on the other

hand, grew up when ______________________________

____

and my values are ____

____

____

____

____

____

____

____.

The following table gives categories to describe your present personality in relation to your parents. Filling in the table may help you make this comparison more detailed. It might help you see yourself more clearly than ever before.

After you've filled in the table, the next step is to look to the future. Now that you have described who you are, at least in terms of similarities and differences from your parents, the questions are, Who do you want to be? What image of your personality will guide you? Who are you trying to become? Which of the characteristics would you like to leave behind? Which would you like to develop? What characteristics that do not appear on the table would you like to add? Use the table on page 112 to help you imagine a new self you would like to be, and use this, as Aristotle says, as a "target to guide [your] actions."

I've left the categories exactly the same as in the first table, although I'm not sure exactly what "ideal" fears and worries might be. Perhaps there are some useful things to worry about, as opposed to the foolish things we normally worry about.

A Portrait of my Personality

Goals	
Values	
Habits	
Strengths	
Sense of Humor	
Idiosyncrasies	
Needs	
Fears/Worries	

A Portrait of my Ideal Personality

Goals	
Values	
Habits	
Strengths	
Sense of Humor	
Idiosyncrasies	
Needs	
Fears/Worries	

·19· A CHILD THINKS ABOUT THE WORLD

Let's see if we can go further into your childhood personality. What were your thoughts and feelings as a child? Let's say you are lying in bed on a summer night long ago. It's hot and you can't sleep. What would be going through your head? Thinking about your father or mother, brothers, sisters, games, or school, what images would you see? For example, if you think of school starting in a month or so, what do you feel?

I am lying in bed in my Home in ______________________________

____________________ . I am ____________________ years old. I stare up into the darkness. Sleep will not come. I kick all the covers away from me. I begin to think about the next school year. I see images of ______________

____

____ . And I feel ________________

____

____

____.

I will try thinking about school and then my parents and see what else comes to mind. I will let the thoughts flow from one part of my world to another. I am trying to re-create ideas I haven't had for thirty-five years.

Time: Summer night, 1954
Home: Devonshire, St. Louis
Location: My bedroom
Situation: I hear my parents downstairs but they aren't watching anything good on TV. I can't sleep. All the windows are open and it is still too hot. I begin to think.

School. The jungle gym. Playing Space Cadets. My third-grade teacher with bluish gray hair. I'm not in the bottom reading group anymore! We studied Brazil and anacondas and tapirs. I think about the Amazon, the largest river in the world. The Indians who build big huts of reeds and straw. They eat manioc (?)

I like school. I like all the little competitions. Tests. Who can finish a math paper first? I love the number nine. It is so powerful. When you add it to something it kicks that number way up. The number eight is good, but it is not as strong as nine. Five is a good number. When you add it to another five you never have to think what the answer will be. I hate division. You have to try too many times, and when you have a remainder it is messy.

I love baseball cards but I hate playing baseball. I love pitching, but I hate hitting and so I hate baseball. The pitcher is the star. Nothing happens until the pitcher starts things off. My father. He has a big lump on his finger. He hurt his hand at work. He brings home his overalls rolled up every day and I always ask him what is inside. He never gets the idea I want him to hide a present in there . . . (and so my night meditation would continue).

Remember, everything you need to know is inside you. You are the world's greatest authority on your childhood and what it felt like to be you long ago. Cross the line once more between memory and reliving. You may start by remembering what you thought long ago, but you will end by feeling many of the same feelings. Let your thoughts move from topic to topic: father, mother, school, games, friends, relatives, the neighborhood, hopes, fears, goals, needs. You are re-creating the emotional side of your childhood world. Let your feelings guide you. Whatever you felt long ago remains in your heart. You can find it.

If it gets too hot, get up and look at the stars.

A Summer Night

Time: Summer night, ______________________

Home: ______________________

Location: My bedroom

Situation: ______________________

____

____

____

Lying in bed, I start to think about ______________________

____

____

____________________ . I feel ____________________

____

____

____________________________ . (and so you continue)

·20·
A Child Dreams

I may be a poor guide in this chapter, because I cannot remember any of my sleeping dreams from childhood. I do remember fantasies, especially about the future. I will go back to that bed on a summer night and relieve one of my favorite fantasies. Then it will be your turn. Perhaps you can add dreams.

Time: Summer night, 1954
Home: Devonshire, St. Louis
Location: My bedroom
Situation: A fantasy about the big leagues

I lie in bed and think about wearing Yankee pinstripes. The catcher is good old Yogi Berra. Moose Skowron is on first. I put my toe to the rubber. I have to remember not to throw the ball sidearm. My father says I get no speed that way. I get the sign: one finger, fastball. I've got what they call a hopping fastball. Only Bob Feller had one like me. Our fastball hops like it's going upstairs. Stan Musial stands at the plate. It is the World Series between the Cards and the Yankees. I see my dad and mom in the stands. My dad looks at me and holds up two fingers, reminding me how to put my fingers over the top seams on the ball. Musial is in that funny little crouch, he wiggles his hips. Dad says that means he wants to get a hit on the next pitch. I go into my windup slowly. I kick my leg across my body; I see Yogi grinning behind his mask. A runner breaks from third. I ignore him. I whip my arm down across my body, not side-arm. I follow through like I'm supposed to. Musial stares at a third strike. Yogi gets the guy sliding. There is a sound like I never heard before: a hundred thousand people screaming, "Biff!" I hear my mom and dad through all the noise. I tip my cap. I'm a big guy coming down off the mound, and my dad is old. I look at him and grin, and he nods like "Go get 'em next inning, but don't get a swelled head."

Your turn. Try to remember dreams, or re-create any daydreams or fantasies you wish.

Dreams and Fantasy

Time: Summer, ______________________________

Home: ______________________________

Location: My bedroom

Situation: A night of dreams and fantasy

I lie in bed. There is darkness all around, but I am not afraid. I wish I could sleep, but I can't. I think about dreams I have had. I think about ________

____

____

____

____

______________________________ . When I think about my dreams

I feel ____

____

____

__________________________ . Now I think about what I would really

like to be someday. I imagine I am ______________________

____

____________________________________ . (and so you continue).

____

____

____

____

____

____

____

Two simple but useful questions: First, is there anything you had fantasies about as a child that is still part of your fantasy life today?

The truth is ____

____

____.

Second, is there any part of your childhood fantasy life you want to use as a guide to your future?

I have to say ____

____

because ____

____

____

____

____

____

____

____

____

·21· INTERLUDE: THE MISSING PIECES

You are beginning to recognize how much there is to discover in your childhood memories. This chapter contains suggestions for additional explorations. You may have been waiting for me to deal with some part of your childhood that I haven't mentioned yet. This is the occasion for you to fill in any pieces I have missed.

Perhaps you want to remember your mother's cooking, or think about your grandmother's house, or hold a dialogue with your sister. There may be subjects that were part of the inner world of your childhood that I cannot imagine.

Circle any of the following you want to spend more time on, or add your own missing pieces.

Possible Missing Pieces

1. Another important house or other place besides your Home (your grandparents'? Your friend's? A store?)
2. An important person I haven't mentioned (relatives, next-door neighbor, teacher, friends of your parents, a bully, someone you loved from afar?)
3. Food

4. Christmas, birthdays, Thanksgiving
5. Summer camp or a visit to the farm, beach, mountains, lake, desert
6. How things smelled, felt, or sounded; the colors of childhood
7. Clothes (your best clothes, favorite clothes, or your parents' clothes)
8. Inside closets, drawers, glove compartments, bureaus
9. Candy (a whole separate world from #3!)
10. Music (I remember tap-dancing to "Stars and Stripes Forever" from a radio big as a closet)
11. Music or dance lessons, or other special classes
12. Clubs
13. Church or other religious groups
14. Going downtown or going shopping
15. The old family car (remember going for a drive?)
16. Or . . .

At this point you know several ways to return to childhood and revive your memories. Make a list of what you see. Hold an "interview." Make a memory picture. Draw a map. Set up a situation and enter it. Or simply write about your memories. Use any of these methods to fill in the missing pieces. (If you haven't done so already, this might be a good occasion to extend this book into your own journal.)

RECOVERING MISSING PIECES OF MY CHILDHOOD

____

____

____

·22·
Old Lessons of Childhood

What we have done in earlier chapters has prepared us for the next three. First, we are going to re-create the lessons our parents taught us about ourselves and the world. Then we are going to examine these lessons critically to see which still seem valuable and which need to be revised or replaced. Finally, we will decide whether it would be useful to deal with painful memories from childhood.

We learned lessons every day of childhood about love and life and the world. Everything our parents did and said created an emotional and intellectual environment that we absorbed continuously. The most important lessons were rarely if ever stated explicitly; our parents did not sit us down and tell us, once and for all, the Truth about the human condition. In general, we learned unconsciously as children whether the world was fundamentally good or bad, fair or unfair; whether we as individuals were competent, incompetent, lovable, difficult, trustworthy or worthless; whether other people should be sought out or shunned, loved or rejected. In this chapter we will recover these lessons; in the next chapter, we will evaluate their truth for us as adults.

Our journey in this book is based on two ideas: the simple idea that our past shaped our present, and the not-so-simple idea that by reliving our past we can find a new path into the future. Many philosophers since Kant would agree that we do not live in the world itself but in our version of the world.

And many psychologists since Freud would agree that our version of the world is shaped in powerful and often idiosyncratic ways by what happened to us in childhood.

Our attention on this journey, however, has not been focused on traumas, the great cataclysms of childhood, but upon daily life. What we experienced as part of our normal routine, the way our parents behaved toward us most of the time, the most general and typical experiences of our childhood, probably had more to do with our present personalities than the dark islands of fear some psychologists would have us search for. In this chapter we want to get at these general truths we absorbed from our parents, the unstated philosophy that was the foundation of our childhood. Let's start with our parents' conception of the Good Life.

From my father's point of view, the Good Life centered around steady employment. He had no other ambition. The Good Life did not involve advancement, special possessions, regular attendance at church, or time for a hobby.

From my mother's point of view, the Good Life involved arts and crafts. What she wanted from life was not a regular job but the time to make things with her hands. The Good Life involved good food to eat and interesting objects for the house. The Good Life also meant travel, advancement, new stimulation. Ultimately, for her, no part of the Good Life was possible outside the borders of California.

The Good Life for my father involved doing the same things over and over, a comfortable routine. The Good Life for my mother involved living like a gypsy.

Your turn.

For my father, the Good Life meant ______________________________

____

____

____

____

For my mother, the Good Life meant _______________________

____

____

____

____

____ .

What our parents taught us about ourselves is the source of our self-image. But this can be confusing if each parent taught us something different. Thus the next question is, What lessons did each of your parents teach you about yourself?

My father taught me that I was inadequate, and in relation to my mother I felt inadequate. I could not pitch well enough for my father, and, in comparison with my mother, I felt as artistic as a chimp. I drew like an eight-year-old and felt awful about it. Most of what my father and I did together was to practice pitching, half an hour a day every day, and day after day I learned I didn't have the stuff. I can't remember doing much with my mother except being the audience for her wonders.

Your turn.

What I learned about myself from my father was _______________

What I learned about myself from my mother was

The next question is, What did they teach you about love?

Perhaps I was too hard on them. They both loved me, no doubt about that, and intensely, each in their own way. They taught me I was lovable. I remember them kissing in the kitchen every day after my father came home from work, and I would try to horn in between their bodies. They taught me that men and women can be good to each other and faithful and not cruel. I remember no fights. But their divorce was a mystery. It came as a surprise announcement.

They may have taught me, without intending to, that love is not forever and that it can end without warning. I think I learned that lesson much more clearly when I lived with my mother after the divorce. Being in love is having a series of relationships, intense but finite. My parents were both physical. I can remember kissing my father good-night and his enjoying it. I can remember being on my mother's lap a lot. They taught me to show affection. But they also taught me that loving worlds come to an end.

Your turn.

What my mother taught me about love was ______

What my father taught me about love was

Now we are ready to think about two other big lessons: the Good Person and the Bad Person. If both your parents shared the same religion and values, these lessons may be easy for you to recall. Nonetheless, there is probably a sense in which the Good and Bad Person extends beyond even the broadest religious categories. Our parents control even the most trivial parts of our existence: a Good Person brushes his hair, a Bad Person lets the screen door slam, a Good Person eats his peas, a Bad Person mumbles. As a child you moved back and forth between the regions of light, where you were smiled upon by your parents, and the regions of darkness, which brought frowns or worse. You heard your parents talking about other people, praising some, scorning others. Occasionally one parent may have represented the other as a Good or Bad Person. What can we teach ourselves now as adults about the lessons we learned long ago as children?

According to my father, a Bad Person was: lazy, cowardly, swell-headed, a "bum." A Good Person, at least from my point of view as a child, was: a good fistfighter, a major leaguer, a good worker, not a crybaby, self-controlled, sensible with money.

From my mother's point of view, a Bad Person . . . (I'm having trouble remembering here. I have to go forward a few years from 1954 because when we lived together after the divorce, I got a much clearer idea of her values.) A Bad Person was a drinker who became mean. Good drinkers stayed happy. A bad drinker got nasty, broke things, was crazy, cruel. A Bad Person was negative. *Negative* was her favorite word for a Bad Person. Bad People thought negative thoughts and thus made bad things happen to themselves. Bad People were always looking on the dark side of things. They deserved what happened to them. A Good Person was psychic. A Good Person knew the future and let the Higher Powers run life. A Good Person was creative, fun loving, adventurous, unconventional, a madcap, a real character. A Good Person was patriotic.

Take your time. Let your parents' beliefs about the Good and Bad Person come back from any part of your childhood.

My Parents' Lessons About the Good Person and the Bad Person

·23·
New Lessons from Childhood

I can certainly see how my parents' ideas about life influenced me. Perhaps if they could read the previous chapter, they might disagree with my impressions. They might say their beliefs were completely different from the ones I remember. But the values I described, as nearly as I can tell, were the ones I absorbed. Maybe in some childish way I made them up and attached these ideas incorrectly to my parents. That really doesn't matter now. These ideas about love and self and the Good Life shaped my whole life. And now I question their usefulness.

When I see some of the ideas I absorbed from my parents, I wish I could strike them out of my head. These values didn't give me an unhappy childhood, but they made me unhappy as a teenager and young adult. I know my parents meant me no harm. They loved me passionately and deeply. They were just being themselves; they were probably teaching me the lessons they learned in their own childhoods. I don't think I was at fault either. Even if I distorted their lessons, I can see no other way I could have behaved or believed then. However, the important point is that I can behave differently now.

We can repeat the past or we can reject it. Every morning when you follow the same routine and get up and go to work, you have decided to carry a useful set of behaviors from the past into the present. When you decide you are completely tired of your job, you reject the past and begin the search for a new world. Similarly, you can decide which lessons from the past merit preservation and which should be left behind.

This is a crucial time in our journey because we are going to part company temporarily. I'm not going to give you examples of the new lessons I want to teach myself. This is a moment for you to be on your own. Your new lessons, if you decide you need them, will have to come entirely from your own reflections; they will not repeat your parents' values, nor should they be influenced by any samples I set before you.

Think about and reread what you wrote in the last chapter about the lessons you learned from your parents. Decide what parts, if any, are wise and what parts, if any, are foolish. If you decide you need to tell yourself new truths about yourself, the world, love, work, or the Good or Bad Person, then do so.

New Lessons I Need to Teach Myself

·24·
Painful Memories

Before you go further in this chapter, decide if you want to explore painful parts of your childhood. If you do, think about which aspects need your attention. If you decide this chapter will not be useful, then take that Wisdom, guilt free, to the next chapter.

My decision is ____

because ____

____

____

____.

Our goal is modest: We want to give ourselves good advice. The odds are that nothing we can do in this book will permanently stop lifelong pain. Any grief that has lasted since childhood has become a habit.

Aristotle recognized the relationship between habit and right actions. In order to become virtuous, he tells us, we must do virtuous things. Our new virtuous actions will build up virtuous habits, which will make it easier to act in the right way. In essence, he argues for building a kind of virtuous feedback loop: Good actions build good habits, and good habits then promote good actions. For Aristotle, the important point is that habits are built from nothing but our actions; habits are not innate or permanently fixed by nature. The connection between habit and action *starts* with action.

This chapter will offer some concrete suggestions for breaking the habit of pain and building the habit of healing. And, following Aristotle, we must begin to build our new habit with some specific healing actions.

The process involves three steps. First we will record a painful memory. Then we will see what healing lessons we can teach ourselves in the present as a result of this painful experience from the past. Finally, we will sketch out some healing actions for the future.

Notice that the whole process is short. This chapter is not built on the catharsis model. I don't believe you are going to get something "out of your system" by writing about it. What is essential is not what we write down, but what we *do* afterward. And whatever we do will have to be repeated, in some form, over and over for us to build healing habits.

I will go through the writing process with you once, and then you can repeat it as often as you wish.

Step 1. Record a painful memory. I will never forget the moment my father told me I was going to be the man of the family. We were in the upstairs living room, and he knelt down to my level and said he and my mother were going to live apart. I told him that my mother had already told me so. I hate that part. He was out of the family already—my mother and I were together, and he didn't even get to be the one to tell me he wouldn't be around anymore. I hate that memory. I feel so much grief for my father. I feel grief for myself, but more for him. He lived alone for the rest of his life. He was alone even before he told me.

Step 2. Look for a healing lesson. This is difficult. We can learn something from every part of our past, however, and the most painful parts should be especially instructive because, if nothing else, they teach us something about our own resiliency.

A few ideas occur to me. Whenever I remember the pain of that moment, I will also try to remember two things: My father survived and I survived. But the sweet and strong idea I have is his survival. He lived alone for 16 years after that and died without a complaint. I love that toughness in him, that hardness that could take a rotten deal and go on. That is what is lovely to me about the old notion of manhood. One may be wounded to the soul, but one endures.

The lesson is simple and obvious: Pain does not quench life. Nietzsche argues that "the bone always mends stronger where it was broken." I would state it less heroically: Walking with a limp is still walking.

Step 3. Try to turn this lesson into a healing habit. I have learned something. The pain I feel in this memory is the pain of separation—separation from my father, and also my father's separation from my mother and myself. If my father were alive, one obvious healing action would be to make it a habit to call or visit him regularly. But in my life now, I should spend more time with my own family. There I can easily recover from the pain of being alone long ago and, more importantly, avoid inflicting it on others. If I could not hold my childhood family together, I can do whatever a father and husband can do to hold his own household together.

Don't expect the healing actions that you discover to be extraordinary. If they are to become habits, they should be common sense and easily adaptable to daily life. What is healing often is not profound. In fact, if we are looking for the profound or hidden, we may fail to find healing actions. We should be willing to do what is obviously good for us and not shun it because it is obvious. We may crave the thrill of finding esoteric answers—perhaps as an escape from the difficulty of *doing* what is obviously and immediately healthy. The difficulty is not in writing down healing actions but in performing them.

Now, if you choose to, recall one or more painful memories by writing them

out, as I have, and look for a healing lesson in them. The healing lesson can be simply that although the experience was horrible, something in you is beautiful and strong because you're still here and moving forward. You are in such good shape that you are trying to find something useful in even the worst experience of your childhood. Next, give yourself some advice about the future. What healing actions should you take? And what is the link between these actions and your painful memory?

·25·
The Wisdom Letter

At the end of Part 1, you created a Silent Reverie over your past. Now, near the end of Part 2, you will write a Wisdom Letter to yourself about your past, present, and future. In doing this, you will bring together everything you have learned along your journey.

First, go back and read everything you have written so far, adding anything you wish. In coming this far, you have traveled a long way. A whole world lies behind this page. Looking through it again will lead you even deeper into it.

After reading the long meditation you created, you are ready to begin your Wisdom Letter. Sum up everything you want to remember from your childhood about yourself, your parents, and other important people. Tell yourself the lessons you learned about your past and give yourself advice about what was healthy and harmful in your heart long ago.

Then think about who you are now. In what sense are you still your father? In what sense are you acting out your father's image of who you are? Is this good or bad for you? In what sense are you still your mother? In what sense are you acting out your mother's image of who you are?

And who are you now? Think of the different aspects of your life: work, family, play, dreams, friendship. Who are you in each of these roles and arenas? In what positive sense have you continued your childhood and in what negative sense?

Then think about your future. Are you living your parents' goals for you or your own? Do you need to find your own? What have you learned from your journey that establishes signposts on the path ahead?

Let your own image of the Good Person show you what to seek and your image of the Bad Person show you what to avoid. You seek only one path, the path of healing. What specific actions will lead you forward? How will you build healing habits?

Write slowly and thoughtfully. At this time you might go back through your starred observations.

Now is the time to bring everything together.

A Wisdom Letter to Myself About My Past, Present, and Future

Date: ______________________________

Dear ______________________________

____

____

____

____

____

____

____

____

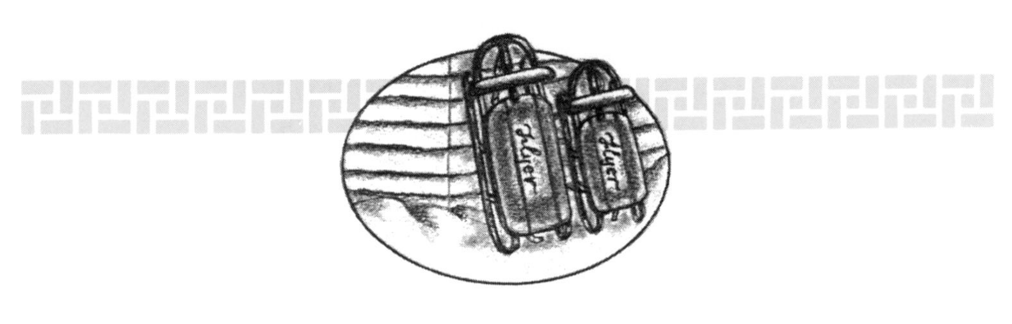

·26·
THE TIME COMPASS

Now you need a device to guide you on your journey alone. Having learned how to investigate a particular period from your childhood, you will wish to search through other years. You might wish to move on to adolescence or any other period you want to see more clearly. Obviously, you can adapt the devices you already used in this book. In addition, you might enjoy experimenting with the Time Compass. This is the gift I promised you in the first chapter. You can use it to visit any place and time.

The Time Compass is made of pen and paper and the images inside your mind. You've already used a version of it in various places on your journey. You simply set the Compass at a particular time and place and call forth the memories of what you see and feel. You can include maps, memory photos, interviews, and healing lessons to bring your experience to vivid life.

Here are several settings on the Time Compass I would use to continue my own journey.

Time: June 1963
City: Sunnyvale, California
Weather: Clear, warm
Location: The bleachers at Sunnyvale High School

Situation: Graduation from high school. I am sitting in the bleachers in my cap and gown with my class.
I see: My mother sitting in the audience, the bleachers on the other side of the field, trees above the school
I feel: Excited . . . daring . . . like doing something silly

(Then I would write about what happens when reliving this moment.)

Time: October 1978
City: San Bernardino, California
Weather: Clear, warm
Location: The handball courts at Valley College
Situation: I am playing racquetball with a student and go outside the courts to get the ball.
I see: My future wife for the first time, standing with her twin sister
I feel: Embarrassed, smitten, shy, excited, stunned

(Again, using this world that the Time Compass re-creates, I would write about what I feel when reliving these important moments.)

Time: 1946
City: St. Louis, Missouri
Weather: Clear
Location: My crib, upstairs in some house with a sloping ceiling
Situation: I am an infant; this is my earliest memory
I see: A room with wallpaper, an upstairs window, the bars on the crib
I feel: Enclosed, wondering

(Beginning with this memory and moving forward through my life, I could construct a brief Wisdom Autobiography. I would set the Time Compass for each crossroad or important event. When I was finished, I would have a record of the great changes in my life.)

Your turn. Set the Time Compass for some place and time in your life.

A Setting on the Time Compass for Future Explorations

Time: ______________________________

City: ______________________________

Weather: ______________________________

Location: ______________________________

Situation: ______________________________

____

____

I see: ______________________________

____

____

I feel: ______________________________

____

____

What happens is: ______________________________

____

You may want to share the world you re-created in this book with someone else. Or you could use the techniques in this book to help a young person keep his or her memories alive. Or you could go back and expand the shorter entries in your journal.

The wisest thing for me to do next would be to ______________________

____

____.

____

____

____

____

____

____

____

____

In the following appendices I have included suggestions for using *A Journey Through Your Childhood* as part of an English curriculum and for writers and therapists.

I wish you well on the path ahead. If you have suggestions, advice, or any comments you would like to share, I would be happy to hear from you. There is no last chapter. Carry on our conversation by writing to me.

Christopher Biffle
Philosophy Department
San Bernardino Valley College
San Bernardino, California 92410

APPENDIX A
For Writing Teachers

Writing doesn't come any more naturally to my philosophy students than to your English students. I think you will recognize much of what the reader does in this book as pre-writing. My students need suggestions about how to get started. In one sense, this book is nothing but, chapter after chapter, beginnings for longer essays.

Here is a list of ways this journey could be used as part of a writing program.

1. The book could be used as the first unit of the program. Most students have an easier time writing about themselves than anything else.
2. Chapters of the book could be coordinated with a selection of autobiographical readings. Students might construct accounts of their own childhood while reading Tolstoy's *Childhood, Boyhood and Youth,* or Maya Angelou's *I Know Why the Caged Bird Sings,* or James Joyce's *Portrait of the Artist as a Young Man,* or an anthology of autobiographical writings. In addition, students could read each other's work.
3. The first half of the book, the Outer World of Childhood, could be used as a series of pre-writing exercises leading up to a full essay, "A Silent Reverie on Childhood." The second half of the book, the Inner World of

Childhood, could be used as a series of pre-writing exercises for "The Wisdom Letter."

4. You could use your own responses to this book as additional samples of the kind of work you are looking for from students. In general, I think teachers don't give students enough samples of their own writing. In addition, you could share with students the pleasures and difficulties of your own journey through this book. This would give them some sense of what to expect and might create a real feeling of community: writers moving toward Wisdom together.
5. The book could form a self-contained writing task to be used as a supplement to in-class work. Formal work could be done in class; the journey could be assigned as a self-guided journal. Students could use the book for extra credit or as a semester project.
6. I believe this text would be especially helpful in teaching English as a second language and in classes for less fluent writers. I hope that this journey demonstrates that writing can be personally helpful. A good idea might be to have students do all the writing in-class, adding your own pre- and post-writing exercises, discussions, and aids.
7. A different tack would be to assign students this book to use as a sourcebook for interviews. Instead of writing about themselves, students could find someone else to guide along a journey of recollection, and then sum up their memories in an essay.
8. Along this same line, a student could use a single chapter as a source for two interviews and then write a comparison/contrast paper.

If you decide to use *A Journey Through Your Childhood* as part of a writing program, please let me know about your experience.

·APPENDIX B·

FOR WRITERS

Childhood is a fertile source for poets and novelists. Theodore Roethke was a skilled but undistinguished poet until he began to write about his childhood experiences in his father's greenhouses. If great poems could be written about the "largest greenhouses in Saginaw, Michigan," they can be written about any childhood experience.

I have written poetry for the last twenty-five years. I don't think I wrote anything worthwhile for the first fifteen. I was writing "poetry" and being "poetic." I wrote about "Nature." Then I started to write about a subject I knew inside out . . . Little League baseball. I found a language that was my own.

Your childhood also makes you expert in something. It may not seem special to you because you know it so well. But you can turn it into poetry or fiction that *only you could write.* Something great can be woven out of any material. James Agee wrote a wondrous book, *Let Us Now Praise Famous Men* about a three-week visit with Southern sharecroppers. He has pages on the smell of pork rind, the light on the outside of a wood shack, the various ages in the life of overalls. Thus, my first suggestion is to use this journey as source material. Find your best material in the smallest, most worn and familiar facts of your childhood.

If you are a writer of fiction, use this book as a source for several characters. If you could imagine how one of your characters would complete this journey, you would know that character very intimately. If you could see how several characters would construct their childhoods differently, you might have the seeds of a great novel. Ivan Turgenev said a good writer knows his characters down to their shoe size. Imagining the way your characters would complete this book, you would know them down to what they kept in the darkest corner of their childhood closets.

• A P P E N D I X C •

For Therapists

I have had a nonprofessional's interest in psychology for several years, and in this and other books I have tried to set forth some techniques for self-analysis. I have attempted to keep my work free of any particular theory of personality or therapy. I want to set up frameworks for self-analysis that a Jungian, Freudian, or Rogerian would be able to adapt to his or her perspective. I want to make tools that any hand can use.

Here are several suggestions for using *A Journey Through Your Childhood* in individual or group therapy.

1. Because you would be using this book in a controlled situation, clients would not have to save their painful memories for one particular chapter. In fact, you may want to include a section of every chapter to deal with the painful or traumatic. For example, you might ask your client to include locations of painful memories in sketching the Home floor plan and neighborhood map. You might suggest more pointed questions that could be asked of parents in the interview (chapter 16), or ask your client to construct a set of memory photographs that include his or her most painful memories.
2. On the subject of memory photographs, I suggest making copies of the photographs page (chapter 15) and using it several times. One set could be about happy memories, another about sad ones, another about mem-

ories of father, another about memories of mother, another about games, and so on. Each page would focus on a particular aspect or leitmotif of childhood. Putting all the memory photographs together might be a powerful way for your client to gain an overview of his or her life.

3. I would also suggest introducing the idea of healing lessons and new habits much earlier than chapter 24. Sessions might begin by talking about which new habit the patient had tried since the last meeting.
4. Group therapy is obviously a fertile occasion for talking about childhood. One advantage of this book is that it provides an ideal set of homework exercises. Group meetings will probably be more fruitful if each client completes written work between the sessions.
5. One way for a husband and wife to begin marriage counseling in a nonconfrontational way would be for them to use this book to learn more about each other's childhood. The partners would begin to see that a central task of each counseling session is mutual understanding.
6. Unresponsive clients might be encouraged to share their experiences if the therapist was involved in, or had been involved in, the same process. As chapter introductions, the therapist might share his or her difficulties or rewards with each exercise.
7. Material completed between therapeutic sessions could be amplified during the sessions by asking patients to talk or write more about particular points. The book could be tailored to each client's needs by suggesting extended journal entries to amplify important chapters.
8. Free association, visualization, and other techniques could be used at appropriate parts of the journey to help clients overcome memory blocks or deepen understanding.
9. The Time Compass in the last chapter could be used, along with techniques like map making, interviews, and memory photographs, to guide a client into an analysis of other periods of life besides childhood. These techniques can be as useful in clarifying the recent as well as the distant past.

NOTES